I CAN'T COOK

SONIA ALLISON

Illustrated by Brian Bagnall

ELM TREE BOOKS . LONDON

By the same author
A PLEASURE TO COOK
COOKING IN STYLE

First published in Great Britain 1983
by Elm Tree Books Ltd
Garden House 57-59 Long Acre London WC2E 9JZ

Copyright © 1983 by Sonia Allison
Illustrations copyright © by Brian Bagnall

British Library Cataloguing in Publication Data

Allison, Sonia
  I can't cook.
  I. Title
  641.5   TX717

  ISBN 0-241-11124-2

Typeset by Pioneer, East Sussex
Printed in Great Britain by
Richard Clay, The Chaucer Press, Bungay, Suffolk

Contents

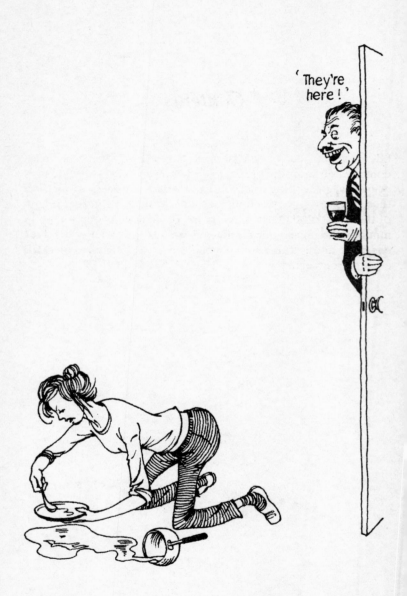

Starters

OK — so you can't cook starters. You can't be bothered with complicated soups that seem to go wrong anyway, your attempts at pâté are revolting and you can't serve up melon *again*. Try these recipes — they're delicious, colourful and different; many of them are ridiculously easy, many of them can be made up in minutes. Astonish your family and friends with your new-found expertise and imagination — you'll never have to say you can't cook starters again!

Arabian Nights
Minted Cucumber Soup

Serves 6 to 8

One of my short-cut ideas where canned condensed soup is gainfully employed to produce an authentic-tasting chilled soup from the Middle East. It's blissful on hot summer days.

1 can condensed cream of chicken soup
10oz (275g) natural yogurt
4 tblsp fresh lemon juice, strained
2 garlic cloves, peeled
¾pt (425 ml) cold water
4oz (125g) unpeeled but washed and dried cucumber, cut into very thin slices
1 level tblsp finely-chopped fresh mint or 2 level tsp bottled (the kind used for mint sauce)
salt and pepper to taste

1. Spoon soup into a bowl then beat in yogurt and lemon juice.
2. Crush garlic and add with cold water, cucumber and mint. Season to taste with salt and pepper.
3. Cover. Refrigerate a minimum of 2 hours. Before serving, stir round and ladle into soup bowls. Accompany with Greek-style bread with sesame seeds or Pitta bread.

'I just hope it's cooking oil'

Russian Borshch   *Serves 6 to 8 generously*

The classic beetroot soup from South Russia, with a distinctive flavour and rich, ruby colour. There are countless recipes and countless families prepared to pass them on, but this version has always been successful for me and is wonderfully sustaining in the depths of winter. A chilled version follows.

1¾pt (1 litre) beef stock (use cubes and water)
1lb (450g) cooked beetroot, peeled and grated
6oz (175g) onions, peeled and grated
4oz (125g) carrots, peeled and grated
8oz (225g) white cabbage, washed and shredded
1 large scrubbed celery stalk, cut into very thin strips
2oz (50g) *each*, peeled swede, turnip and parsnip, finely grated
1 level tblsp tubed or canned tomato purée
juice of a small lemon
1 rounded tsp brown sugar
seasoning to taste
2 rounded tblsp chopped parsley or fresh dill for garnishing
soured cream

1. Put beef stock into saucepan. Add 12oz (350g) beetroot, onions, carrots, white cabbage, celery, swede, turnip, parsnip and purée.
2. Bring to boil, stirring. Lower heat and cover. Simmer ½ hour.
3. Stir in lemon juice, rest of beetroot (at this point soup will change from a sallow red to a bright red) and sugar. Stir round and season to taste.
4. Ladle into soup bowls and sprinkle each with parsley or dill. Top each with 2 heaped teaspoons soured cream and accompany with black bread.

Chilled Beetroot Soup   *Serves 6 to 8 generously*

Make exactly as previous recipe. After simmering for ½ hour,
strain soup into a clean pan. Add rest of beetroot, lemon juice
and sugar. Cover. Chill at least 4 hours in the refrigerator. Stir
round before serving and ladle into soup bowls. Top each with
soured cream.

Blender Beetroot and   *Serves 8*
Tomato Soup

Use a blender or food processor and you will have instant
success with this distinctively-flavoured chilled soup, distantly
related to Borshch.

1½lb (675g) cooked beetroots
Ilb (450g) tomatoes, blanched and skinned
2 level tsp salt
2oz (50g) onion, peeled and cut into eighths
2 garlic cloves, peeled and halved
1 tblsp cider or wine vinegar
1pt (575ml) cold water
8 heaped tsp soured cream

1. Peel beetroots and cut into large cubes. Cut tomatoes into
   wedges. Toss with salt, onion and garlic.
2. Put into blender or food processor, in 2 or 3 batches, and run
   machine until mixture is very smooth.
3. Transfer to mixing bowl and gently whisk in vinegar and
   water. Cover. Chill for a minimum of 4 hours. Stir round
   before serving.
4. Ladle into bowls and top each with soured cream.

Speedy Vichyssoise

Serves 6 to 8

This version of Vichyssoise breaks through all the time barriers
yet it has a classy taste and authentic appearance; ideal summer
eating.

1 large packet instant mashed potato powder or flakes
2pt (1¼ litre) boiling water
3 to 4 level tsp onion salt
½pt (275ml) double cream
Garnish
about 6 to 8 heaped tblsp scissor-snipped chives or very finely-
  chopped green part of leek

1. Tip instant potato powder or flakes into a bowl. Add onion
   salt.
2. Gradually blend in the boiling water. Cool. Cover. When
   completely cold, refrigerate several hours or until well-chilled.
3. Before serving, gently whisk in cream. Ladle into bowls and
   sprinkle each with chives or leek.

Quick Carrot Soup

Serves 4

A no-hassle soup for those occasions when you are in a hurry
for homemade 'fast food'.

1 large can of carrots, drained
¾pt (425ml) chicken stock (use cubes and water)
¼pt (150ml) single cream
2 tblsp sweet sherry
1 tsp lemon juice
freshly-milled black pepper
chopped parsley for garnishing

1. Put carrots, stock, cream, sherry and lemon juice into blender and run machine until smooth.
2. Pour into pan, heat gently until hot then season to taste with pepper. Ladle into soup bowls and sprinkle with parsley. Serve with cheese biscuits below.

Cheese Biscuits

Makes about 20

4oz (125g) plain flour
pinch *each* of salt and powder mustard
pinch of cayenne pepper (optional)
2oz (50g) Dutch unsalted butter
2oz (50g) Edam cheese, grated
1 Grade 3 egg yolk
2 to 3 tsp cold water

1. Sift dry ingredients into bowl and rub in butter finely. Toss in cheese then mix to a semi-stiff dough with egg yolk and water.
2. Knead quickly until smooth on floured surface, roll out fairly thinly then cut into 1½in (3¾cm) rounds with biscuit cutter, re-rolling and re-cutting trimmings to make required amount.
3. Transfer to baking tray. Bake 12 to 15 minutes just above oven centre set to 200°C (400°F), Gas 6. Cool on a wire rack and store in airtight tin when cold.

Andalusian Gazpacho

Serves 6

Spain's foremost chilled soup and a colourful blend of popular ingredients. Like curries, it is served with its own accompaniments which are given further down.

1 garlic clove, peeled
1 small washed green pepper, quartered and de-seeded
1 small washed red pepper, quartered and de-seeded
1½lb (675g) very red blanched tomatoes, skinned and quartered
4 level tblsp tubed or canned tomato purée
1 large onion, peeled and cut into eighths
2 level tblsp icing sugar, sifted
4 tblsp corn or olive oil (the latter has a stronger taste)
3 tblsp wine or cider vinegar
crumbs from 4 large slices white bread, with crusts removed first
½pt (275ml) cold water
salt and pepper to taste

Accompaniments
Put the following into separate bowls so that people can help themselves to all or some of the accompaniments. Make sure there is a spoon in each:
1. Unpeeled cucumber, cut into tiny dice
2. Half a small red pepper, washed and de-seeded then cut into tiny dice
3. 1 medium onion, peeled and fairly finely chopped
4. 2 hard-boiled eggs (large), shelled and chopped or grated
5. 2 slices white bread, cut into tiny cubes then fried in oil or butter

Soup
1. Blend garlic, peppers, tomatoes, purée and onion, in two batches, in blender goblet or food processor until smooth.
2. Tip into mixing bowl. Gently beat in rest of ingredients.

13

Cover and refrigerate a minimum of 6 hours.
3. To serve, stir round and ladle into bowls. Serve with the accompaniments.

Tomato and Avocado Swirl Soup

Serves 4

A subtle tomato soup, laced with apricot brandy and made grander by the addition of a delicate avocado purée, swirled in at the last minute. It is also very simple and quick to prepare.

1 can condensed tomato soup
½pt (275ml) water
3 medium blanched tomatoes, skinned and cut into wedges
½ tsp Worcestershire sauce
1 tblsp apricot brandy

Avocado Purée
1 medium ripe avocado
2 tsp fresh lemon juice
1 rounded tblsp soured cream
½ level tsp onion salt
salt and pepper to taste
cold milk if necessary

1. Tip soup, water, tomato wedges and Worcestershire sauce into a saucepan. Slowly bring to boil, stirring.
2. Stir in apricot brandy. Cover. Keep hot over minimal heat.
3. For avocado purée, halve avocado. Remove stone and scoop flesh into mixing bowl. Mash very finely with lemon juice and soured cream.
4. Beat in onion salt then season to taste with salt and pepper. If purée remains on the thick side, thin down with a little cold milk.
5. Pour hot soup into plates or bowls and swirl in the avocado

mixture. Accompany with toast.

Tip

For a very smooth avocado purée, put all ingredients into a food processor or blender goblet and run either machine until ingredients are smooth.

Accompany with toast

Avgolemono Soup

Serves 6 generously

A simply constructed Greek soup which is based on three principal ingredients — chicken stock, eggs and lemon juice.

3pt (about 1¾ litre) chicken stock made from a chicken carcase
3oz (75g) round grain pudding rice
3 Grade 3 eggs
juice of 2 large lemons, strained
seasoning to taste

1. Pour chicken stock into a large saucepan. Add rice and bring to boil. Cover and simmer until rice is tender, allowing about

15

30 to 40 minutes. Keep heat fairly low.
2. Break eggs into a soup tureen or large bowl. Add lemon juice and beat until frothy.
3. Gradually whisk in chicken stock and rice. Season to taste and serve straight away.

Chinese Egg Thread and Sweetcorn Soup

Serves 6 generously

A speedy soup to prepare and a pleasing starter to a Chinese meal, whether self-made or brought in from a local 'take-away'.

1¾pt (1 litre) chicken stock, made by boiling up a chicken carcase or from stock cubes and water
3oz (75g) cooked chicken, cut into fine strips
3 level tblsp cornflour
4 tblsp cold water
2 Grade 3 eggs, well-beaten
1 tblsp lemon juice
large pinch of granulated sugar
3oz (75g) cooked sweetcorn
seasoning to taste

1. Pour chicken stock into a pan and add chicken. Bring to boil and lower heat. Cover. Simmer for 15 minutes.
2. Mix cornflour smoothly with cold water. Add to stock. Cook, whisking continually, until soup comes up to the boil and thickens slightly.
3. Beat eggs, lemon juice and sugar well together. Trickle into boiling soup and stir until it forms threads.
4. Mix in sweetcorn and reheat briefly. Ladle into bowls and serve plain or with prawn crackers.

Cucumber Cream Soup

Serves 6

One tends to associate cucumber only with salad, yet it responds well to cooking and this soup is a fine example of how versatile it can be. The merest trace of Pernod gives the soup a touch of chic but may be omitted if preferred.

2lb (900g) cucumber, peeled
1½oz (40g) butter or margarine
1½oz (40g) cornflour
1pt (575ml) chicken stock (use cubes and water in the absence the real thing), left to get cold
½pt (275ml) double cream
1½ to 2 level tsp salt
1 tsp Pernod (optional)
white pepper to taste
2 rounded tblsp chopped dill or scissor-snipped chives to decorate

1. Thinly grate cucumber into see-through slices using grater or slicing attachment of food processor. Tip into bowl and cover. Leave to stand 30 minutes so that some of the moisture seeps out.
2. Transfer to a tea towel and wring until cucumber is as dry as possible.
3. Melt butter or margarine in saucepan. Add cucumber and fry gently, covered, for about 7 minutes. Do not allow to brown at all.
4. Mix cornflour smoothly with a little of the stock. Add remainder. Gradually add to cucumber. Cook, stirring, until soup comes to the boil and thickens slightly. Simmer, uncovered, 5 minutes.
5. Stir in cream and season to taste with salt. Mix in Pernod (if used) and pepper. Ladle into soup bowls or plates and sprinkle each with dill or chives.

A perfect soup for inclement weather

Swiss Cheese Soup

Serves 4 to 6

A perfect soup for inclement weather and ideally suited to those who enjoy cheese and wine mixtures which are somewhat reminiscent of fondue.

1oz (25g) butter or margarine
1oz (25g) flour
1pt (575ml) chicken stock
1 garlic clove, peeled
½ level tsp caraway seeds
¼pt (150ml) dry white wine
4oz (125g) Emmenthal cheese, finely grated
¼pt (150ml) hot milk
salt and pepper to taste
chopped parsley for garnishing

1. Melt butter or margarine in a saucepan. Stir in flour to form a roux and cook 1 minute without browning.
2. Gradually add stock. Cook, stirring, until soup comes to the boil and thickens slightly.
3. Crush garlic directly into pan then add caraway seeds and wine.
4. Bring to boil, stirring. Lower heat, cover pan and simmer gently for 10 minutes.
5. Put cheese and milk into a bowl then gradually whisk in hot stock and wine mixture.
6. Season to taste with salt and pepper then ladle into warm soup bowls or cups. Sprinkle with parsley and serve.

Love Apple Spice Soup

Serves 4 to 6

In the old days, tomatoes were known as love apples and looked upon with a measure of suspicion by our Victorian ancestors who must have associated them with subjects one never discussed in the parlour! It is our good fortune that the popularity of love apples has grown or this tangy soup might never have happened!

8oz (225g) washed and dried courgettes, skin left on and grated into thin slices
1pt (575ml) beef stock (use stock cubes and water)
1 can condensed tomato soup
2 tblsp Cointreau
1 tblsp fresh lemon juice
1 level tsp preserved ginger, finely chopped
¼ level tsp allspice

1. Put grated courgettes into a saucepan with beef stock. Bring to boil, stirring. Cover. Simmer 10 to 15 minutes.
2. Stir in tomato soup, Cointreau, lemon juice, ginger and allspice.
3. Bring to boil, again stirring. Simmer, uncovered, for 3 to 4 minutes. Serve with cheese biscuits.

Short-Cut French Onion Soup   *Serves 4*

A lazy way out with a French classic that makes excellent winter eating.

2oz (50g) butter or margarine
1 tblsp salad oil
1lb (450g) frozen sliced onions
1½oz (40g) flour
1¾pt (1 litre) beef stock (use cubes and water)
1 to 1½ level tsp salt
freshly-milled black pepper to taste
4 slices French bread, diagonally cut and 1 in (2½cm) thick

2oz (50g) Gruyère cheese, grated
2oz (50g) Cheddar cheese, grated

1. Heat butter and oil in heavy-based saucepan. Add onions from frozen. Fry briskly at first then reduce heat to medium and continue to fry, turning occasionally, until onions turn a warm goldish-brown.
2. Stir in flour and mix well with the onions. Gradually blend in stock and cook fairly gently until soup thickens slightly and begins to bubble.
3. Add salt and pepper to taste. Cover pan. Simmer soup for about 40 to 50 minutes or until onions are soft.
4. About 5 or 6 minutes before soup is ready, sprinkle bread slices with cheese and brown lightly under a hot grill.
5. Ladle soup into 4 large, warm bowls and top each with a slice of cheese bread. Serve straight away.

Tip
For increased piquancy, spread bread with French mustard before topping with cheese and grilling.

Consommé 'Cocktails'　　　*Serves 4*

An elegant affair, simply made from a basis of canned consommé. If possible, choose conical-shaped cocktail glasses on a short stem so that the layers of the 'cocktail' show through for maximum colour effect.

4 heaped tblsp blanched and skinned tomatoes
4 tsp Worcestershire sauce
4 tsp lemon juice
1 level tsp salt
1 can condensed consommé, left overnight in refrigerator
1 carton (5oz or 142ml) soured cream
1 tblsp cold milk
about 2 rounded tsp finely-grated orange peel

1. Place equal amounts of tomatoes into 4 large cocktail glasses. Sprinkle with Worcestershire sauce, lemon juice and salt.
2. Spoon chilled consommé into glasses on top of tomatoes, spreading it evenly with a knife.
3. Beat soured cream and milk gently together then 'float' on top of consommé. Sprinkle mounds of orange peel on to centres of each. Chill lightly before serving.

To vary
Use grated cucumber instead of tomato, squeezed dry in a cloth. Mix with 1 rounded teaspoon dried dill and 1 level teaspoon salt. Omit Worcestershire sauce and lemon juice. Top cream with 2 or 3 very thin strips of red pepper.

For 8 servings
Double all the ingredients.

Mushroom Caskets
Serves 4

We make too little of raw mushrooms with their subtle, woody taste and versatility. To prove how good they can be, here is one favourite starter, flavoured with garlic and a trace of thyme.

12oz (350mg) button mushrooms, washed and dried
1 garlic clove
½ level tsp finely-grated orange peel
3 tblsp olive oil
1 tblsp lemon juice
½ tblsp cider vinegar
1 level tsp salt
3 rounded tblsp chopped parsley
½ level tsp dried thyme
4 rounded tblsp grated carrots
1 tblsp mayonnaise
1 level tblsp chopped walnuts

1. Thinly slice mushrooms then put into a mixing bowl.
2. Peel garlic and crush directly over mushrooms. Add orange peel.
3. Beat together oil, lemon juice, vinegar, salt, parsley and thyme.
4. Pour over mushrooms and toss gently with a spoon. Cover. Leave to stand 15 minutes for flavours to blend.
5. Transfer to 4 dishes and make a well in each. Fill with the grated carrots, first tossed with the mayonnaise. Sprinkle with walnuts.

Poor Man's 'Caviar'

Serves about 8

Another classic Middle-Eastern dish based on aubergines. It makes an appetising starter to a Balkan or Near East meal.

1½lb (675g) aubergines
4 tblsp lemon juice
6oz (175g) onion, peeled and quartered
1 garlic clove, peeled and sliced
2 tblsp olive oil
1 to 1½ level tsp salt
finely-chopped fresh mint, coriander or parsley for garnishing

1. Wash and dry aubergines but do not peel. Place on a lightly-oiled baking tray and bake until tender when pressed; about 30 minutes in oven at 200°C (400°F), Gas 6. When ready, the skins should split.
2. Remove from oven, rinse under cold water and remove skins. Squeeze aubergines in the hands to remove as much surplus liquid as possible, then cut into thick slices.
3. Put into blender or food processor with lemon juice, onion, garlic and oil.
4. Run machine until ingredients look like a coarse purée. Spoon into a bowl and season to taste with salt. Mound

23

neatly into a serving dish and sprinkle with the mint, coriander or parsley. Serve with Pitta bread.

American-Style Aubergine Dip *Serves 6 to 8*

Prepare aubergines exactly as above. Put into blender or food processor with 4 tablespoons lemon juice and 3oz (75g) cream cheese flavoured with herbs, garlic etc. Run machine until mixture forms a smooth purée. Season to taste with salt and pepper. Put into a bowl or dish and serve with a selection of raw vegetables to include carrot slices, 1½ in (4cm) lengths of celery, cauliflower florets and whole radishes.

Guacamole *Serves 4 to 6*

A Mexican-style dip, served with broken-up pieces of Tortillas which are now available in packets from some supermarket chains. If not, substitute pieces of wafer-thin crispbread.

2 large, ripe avocados
2 tblsp lemon juice
6oz (175g) blanched tomatoes, skinned and very finely chopped
1 small washed and dried green pepper, split and de-seeded then very finely chopped
2oz (50g) onion, peeled and fairly finely grated
1 heaped tblsp finely-chopped fresh coriander or parsley
½ tsp Tabasco
salt to taste

1. Halve avocados, remove stones then spoon flesh into a mixing bowl. Reserve 1 stone.
2. Mash flesh finely with lemon juice, using a stainless fork.
3. Stir in tomatoes, green pepper, onion, coriander or parsley,

Tabasco and salt to taste.
4. Spoon into a serving dish and 'bury' the stone in the middle to prevent avocado mixture from browning. Serve straight away with the pieces of Tortillas or crispbreads.

A Mexican dip

Zatziki

A temperate dip from a hot climate and wonderful in summer with torn pieces of Pitta bread, warmed lightly under the grill.

1½ large cucumbers
salt
10oz (275g) natural yogurt
2 garlic cloves, peeled and crushed
4 tblsp olive oil
2 tblsp fresh lemon juice, strained
2 rounded tsp icing sugar, sifted
3 rounded tblsp soured cream
1 rounded tsp very finely-chopped fresh mint
2 rounded tsp very finely-chopped parsley
salt and pepper to taste

1. Peel cucumbers and grate finely. Put into a large mixing bowl. Sprinkle with salt. Cover. Leave to stand 1½ hours.
2. Drain thoroughly then tip into a tea towel and virtually wring dry. Return to bowl and work in all remaining ingredients. Adjust seasoning to personal taste.
3. To serve, spoon generous amounts on to plates and accompany with warm Pitta bread or Balkan-style white bread sprinkled with sesame seeds.

Hummus

A chick pea and sesame seed mix, served all over the Middle East. It is absolutely delicious, especially scooped on to Pitta bread. A very plain Hummus can also be made without the addition of the sesame seeds, usually bought in paste form (Tahina) from Greek-Cypriot grocers, delicatessens and some of the more enterprising supermarket chains. Both recipes follow.

1 can (14oz or 400g) chick peas, drained
1 garlic clove, peeled and sliced
6 level tblsp Tahina (sesame seed paste)
3 tblsp lemon juice
3 tblsp olive oil
¼pt (150ml) boiling water
salt to taste
extra olive oil
finely-chopped fresh parsley or coriander for garnishing

1. Tip chick peas, garlic, Tahina, lemon juice, olive oil and water into blender goblet or food processor. Run machine until ingredients form a mayonnaise-like consistency.
2. Season to taste then spoon out on to individual plates. Make a dip in the centre of each with the back of a tablespoon then fill with oil in traditional style.
3. Sprinkle portions with parsley or coriander and serve with warm Pitta bread.

Simple Hummus
Serves about 8

Make as recipe above but use 2 cans drained chick peas and omit Tahina paste.

Egg Pâté
Serves 6 to 8

Shaped into a loaf and decorated with a criss-cross of anchovies, this is a kind of glorified egg mayonnaise but more original and

blends very well with an accompaniment of rye bread or
Pumpernickel.

12 Grade 2 eggs, hard-boiled
2 level tblsp scissor-snipped chives
2 level tblsp finely-chopped parsley
2oz (50g) butter, melted
½ to 1 level tsp salt
12 anchovy fillets, canned in oil then drained
black or green stuffed olives
sliced radishes
parsley sprigs

1. Grate eggs directly into a large bowl. Add chives, parsley,
   melted butter and salt. Mix thoroughly.
2. Spoon on to an oblong serving dish and shape into a 2 in
   (5cm) high loaf, wiping dish clean round the loaf with kitchen
   paper.
3. Decorate top with a criss-cross of anchovy fillets then add
   olives and radishes to taste.
4. Outline lower edges of loaf with parsley sprigs then chill
   lightly before spooning on to plates and serving.

Turkey Pâté with Gin   *Serves 6 to 8*

A tantalising-tasting pâté which can be made using tubs of
turkey livers which are readily available from some supermarket
chains. This recipe does need a blender or food processor.

2oz (50g) butter (not margarine for this one)
1 tsp salad oil
6oz (175g) onions, peeled and chopped
1 garlic clove, peeled and sliced
12oz (350g) turkey livers, washed and dried

1½ tblsp gin
salt and pepper to taste

Topping
2oz (50g) butter, melted
about 12 juniper berries

1. Heat butter and oil in a pan. Add onions and garlic. Fry gently until pale gold, allowing 10 to 15 minutes and stirring from time to time.
2. Add livers. Fry over low heat until cooked through, allowing about 30 to 40 minutes and turning fairly often.
3. Blend, with gin and leftover butter from pan, in blender or food processor until mixture forms a smooth purée.
4. Spoon out into a mixing bowl and work in sufficient salt and pepper to taste.
5. Spread smoothly into a smallish dish (tall rather than wide) and float melted butter over the top which, when set, acts as an airtight seal.
6. As soon as butter is firm, stud top with juniper berries then cover dish with clingfilm or foil. Keep in the refrigerator and eat within 1 week of making.
7. To serve, spoon out on to plates and accompany with hot toast.

Not for Snobs Liver Paste

Serves 4, 3 times round

This Liver Paste has no illusions of grandeur and although *I* think it is superb, please do not compare it with French Country pâtés or the sort of Pâté Maison served in bistros and classy hotels. It is infinitely superior and has its rich and creamy roots deep in Scandinavia.

8 oz (225g) chicken livers, washed and dried
8oz (225g) pig's liver, washed and dried then cut into large
  squares
1 medium onion, peeled and cut into eighths
1 garlic clove, peeled and halved (optional)
2oz (50g) plain flour
2oz (50g) butter, melted
1 Grade 2 egg, beaten
1 carton (5 fluid oz or 150ml) double cream
1 tblsp cold milk
¼ level tsp mixed spice
large pinch *each* ground bay and ground mace
1½ level tsp salt
¼ level tsp white pepper

1. Brush a 2lb (1kg) oblong loaf tin with melted butter. Line
   base and sides smoothly with foil and brush with more
   melted butter.
2. Finely mince together the raw livers, onion and garlic (if
   used) or grind smoothly in food processor or blender.
3. Tip into a mixing bowl and gently beat in flour, melted
   butter, egg, cream, milk, spices, salt and pepper.
4. The mixture at this stage will seem very wet and runny but it
   thickens while cooking. Pour into prepared loaf tin.
5. Cover with a length of foil brushed with melted butter. Bake
   for 2 hours in oven set to 180°C (350°F), Gas 4. The Paste is
   ready when a wooden cocktail stick, pushed gently into the
   centre, comes out clean.
6. Remove from oven, cool completely in the tin then uncover.
   Turn out on to a plate and carefully peel away foil.
   Refrigerate until firm and set.
7. Transfer to a board and cut into slices. Arrange 2 per person
   on a lettuce-lined plate. Accompany with freshly-made toast
   and butter.

Smoked Mackerel Pâté

Serves 4

A popular pâté, made from a smoked fish that is now readily available all over the country.

1 can (7oz or 200g) smoked mackerel fillets in oil or brine
6oz (175g) Edam cheese, grated
3oz (75g) Dutch unsalted butter, melted
4 tblsp single cream
2 tblsp whisky
1 level tblsp chopped parsley
2 tsp lemon juice
1 level tsp finely-grated orange peel
salt and pepper to taste
pieces of orange and sprigs of parsley for garnishing

1. Drain mackerel and remove skin. Flake fish with a fork. Beat well with a wooden spoon or blend smoothly in blender or food processor.
2. Beat in cheese with remaining ingredients then season to taste with salt and pepper.
3. Divide the mixture between 4 individual dishes and smooth tops with a damp knife. Chill in the refrigerator 1½ to 3 hours.
4. Garnish with orange and parsley then serve with triangles of hot brown toast.

Double Green Avocado Cocktails

Serves 4

A cool customer for hot days in tones of green and yellows.

2 medium, ripe avocados
4 tblsp corn oil
1 Grade 1 or 2 (large) egg
juice of 1 medium lemon, strained
½ level tsp salt
½ level tsp prepared English mustard
¼ level tsp white pepper
2 tblsp double cream
4 heaped tblsp shredded Cos or Webb lettuce
1 can (about 1lb or 450g) grapefruit segments in natural juice
1oz (25g) almond flakes, lightly toasted
4 sprigs of washed and dried watercress

1. Halve avocados, remove stones and scoop flesh into blender goblet or food processor.
2. Add oil, egg, lemon juice, salt, mustard, pepper and cream. Blend until very smooth.
3. Put lettuce into 4 large wine-type glasses. Drain grapefruit and reserve juice for drinks or cooking. Spoon segments over lettuce.
4. Coat with equal amounts of avocado mixture then sprinkle with almonds. Top each with a sprig of watercress.

Unusual Prawn Cocktails   Serves 4

A very different-from-usual version of the most popular starter in the UK.

Make up the avocado mixture as given in previous recipe but include 2 rounded teaspoons creamed horseradish sauce and ¼ level teaspoon cayenne pepper. Put 4 heaped tablespoons shredded Cos or Webb lettuce into 4 wine-type glasses. Add 1½oz (40g) peeled prawns to each. Cover with the avocado mixture then hang a lemon slice — first slit from centre to outside edge — on to rim of each glass. Dust tops lightly with paprika.

Chicory Vinaigrette with Eggs   *Serves 4*

Chicory is a much under-rated vegetable which deserves to be used more and this sophisticated starter, served lightly chilled, is an elegant example of how this traditional Belgian favourite can be used to create an unusual and fairly inexpensive dish.

8 heads of chicory
1pt (575ml) cold water
3 tsp lemon juice (to keep chicory white)
1 level tsp salt
7 tblsp well-flavoured French dressing
2 Grade 2 eggs, hard-boiled then shelled and chopped
1 rounded tblsp chopped parsley

1. 'Core' each head of chicory by removing a cone-shaped piece from base with a potato peeler. This helps to elminate the bitterness which sometimes characterises chicory.
2. Wash and dry heads, first removing any bruised or damaged outside leaves.
3. Put heads into a large frying pan in single layer. Add water, lemon juice and salt. Bring to boil and cover. Lower heat.
4. Simmer gently for 25 to 30 minutes. Drain very thoroughly by placing chicory in a colander and leaving until cold.
5. Cut each head in half lengthwise and arrange on a large plate. Coat with French dressing then sprinkle with egg. Refrigerate 1 hour before serving.

Turkish Fried Vegetables with Yogurt Sauce   *Serves 4 to 6*

An out-of-the ordinary starter which is ideal if you are having

Typically Turkish and . . . a little on the rich side

any sort of meat or fish kebabs to follow. It is typically Turkish and tastes a little on the rich side, due to the use of olive oil.

1lb (450g) aubergines
salt
4 tblsp olive oil
1 garlic clove, peeled and crushed
2 medium green peppers, washed and dried then de-seeded and
  cut into strips
1lb (450g) *small* blanched tomatoes, skinned

Yogurt Topping
10oz (275g) natural yogurt
2 tblsps cold water
1 garlic clove, peeled
½ to 1 level tsp salt

1. Wash and dry aubergines but do not peel. Cut into ½ in (1¼cm) thick slices. Place on a board in a single layer.
2. Sprinkle heavily with salt and leave to stand for 45 minutes in order to draw out moisture. Turn over, sprinkle with more salt and leave to stand a further 45 minutes.
3. Rinse under cold water and lightly squeeze slices between your hands. Afterwards dry each thoroughly in a tea towel.
4. Heat oil in a large frying pan. Add aubergine slices, a few at a time, and fry fairly briskly on both sides until golden. Remove to crumpled kitchen paper to drain and leave for time being.
5. Add garlic and pepper strips to pan. Cover. Cook gently 10 minutes, stirring twice. Add tomatoes, cover again and cook 5 minutes.
6. Arrange vegetables attractively on a dish. Cover with paper towels and refrigerate until thoroughly chilled.
7. To serve, spoon on to plates and accompany with the yogurt topping, made by beating all ingredients well together.

Different-from-Usual
Egg Mayonnaise

Serves 4

The difference in this recipe is a tangy dressing made by mixing mayonnaise with an equal amount of natural yogurt. It 'lightens' the whole dish, appealing to those who find mayonnaise alone with eggs a little too rich.

8 large lettuce leaves (round lettuce), washed and dried
4 Grade 2 hard-boiled eggs, shelled and halved lengthwise
4 level tblsp thick mayonnaise
4 rounded tblsp natural yogurt
½ level tsp anchovy essence (optional)
1 level tblsp tubed or canned tomato purée
¼ level tsp cayenne pepper

Garnish
8 medium spring onions, trimmed and coarsely chopped
4 medium washed and dried radishes, trimmed and sliced

1. Line 4 bread and butter plates with lettuce. Top each with 2 egg halves, cut sides down.
2. Mix mayonnaise with yogurt, anchovy essence if used, tomato purée and cayenne pepper.
3. Spoon equal amounts over eggs then sprinkle with onions and garnish attractively with radishes. Serve with brown bread and butter.

Smoked Fish with
Scrambled Eggs

Serves 4

Typically Scandinavian in character, this is a very easy starter, as you can see . . .

6 Grade 3 eggs
1oz (25g) butter
2 tblsp milk
salt and pepper to taste
6oz (175g) smoked fish such as salmon, mackerel, eel or trout or
   a mixture of fish
about 4 level tsp fresh chopped dill or parsley

1. Beat eggs then put into a saucepan with butter and milk.
   Season to taste with salt and pepper.
2. Scramble until creamy then set aside to cool. Spoon on to 4
   plates and add pieces of smoked fish as desired.
3. Sprinkle with the chopped dill or parsley and serve with hot
   toast, preferably made from brown bread, and butter.

Orchard Cocktail

Serves 4

An exquisitely refreshing blend of citrus fruits mellowed with
avocados — a guaranteed success story.

2 large grapefruit, pink for preference
2 large oranges
4oz (125g) fresh dates, skinned and halved with stones removed
1 medium, ripe avocado

1. Peel grapefruit and oranges, removing all the white pith.
2. Working over a bowl to catch the juice, cut out segments of
   fruit in between the membranes.
3. Add dates. Peel avocado as you peel a pear, starting from the
   pointed end. Dice flesh. Gently stir into citrus and date
   mixture.
4. Cover. Refrigerate 1 hour. Spoon into wine-type glasses and
   serve.

Pear Flair

Serves 4

A pretty-to-look-at and appetising starter composed of canned pear halves packed with a savoury cottage cheese mix and decorated with redcurrant jelly.

1 small round lettuce, washed and leaves wiped dry
1 large can (1lb 13oz or 822g) pear halves, drained (reserve syrup for drinks, puddings, etc)
1 carton (8oz or 225g) cottage cheese
6 trimmed spring onions, chopped
2oz (50g) salted peanuts, coarsely chopped
½ level tsp finely-grated lemon peel
redcurrant jelly
fresh mint leaves for garnishing

1. Line a serving dish or shallow bowl with the lettuce.
2. Dry pears all over by dabbing with kitchen paper. Stand, cut sides uppermost, on top of lettuce.
3. Mix together cheese, onions, peanuts and lemon peel. Spoon on to pear halves. Top each with ½ teaspoon of redcurrant jelly.
4. Refrigerate 1 hour before serving then garnish with mint leaves. Accompany with brown bread and butter.

Pineapple 'Platters'

Serves 6

Peel a large pineapple and cut into 6 slices. Put on to bread and butter plates. Make up cottage cheese mixture as above and mound on to pineapple slices. Sprinkle with grated carrot then decorate each with unpeeled cucumber, cut into dice. Serve lightly chilled.

Gingered Ogen Melons with Kiwis

Serves 4

Very much for those who are into exotics and enjoy the slightly perfumed flavour of melon, kiwis and ginger.

2 Ogen melons
4 kiwi fruit
2 pieces of preserved ginger in syrup, drained and chopped
ginger wine

1. Halve melon and remove seeds. Peel kiwis and slice. Distribute evenly between the melon hollows then sprinkle with ginger.
2. Cover and refrigerate until well chilled; about 1 hour. Before serving, fill with ginger wine.

Kiwi and Grapefruit Cocktail   *Serves 4*

Garnished with slices of lime, this cool green combination is blissfully refreshing on hot days and looks fashionably elegant served in wine-type glasses on stems.

1 can (about 1lb or 450g) grapefruit segments in natural juice or syrup, depending on taste
2 kiwi fruit, peeled and thinly sliced
4 slices of fresh lime

1. Divide grapefruit segments and kiwi slices between 4 wine-type glasses on stems. Top up with juice or syrup. Refrigerate at least 1 hour.
2. Before serving, make a slit in each slice of lime from centre to outside edge and put on to rim of glass.

Sunset Cocktail   *Serves 4*

Vividly-coloured, this mix of pineapple and pomegranates makes an unusual beginning to any winter meal.

1 medium pineapple
2 large pomegranates
2 tblsp orange-flavoured liqueur
watercress

1. Peel pineapple, slice fairly thinly then cut slices into small triangular-shaped pieces. Do not remove centre core as this is often the most flavoursome and sweetest part of the fruit.
2. Put into mixing bowl. Cut pomegranates into quarters then bend the quarters backwards (skin to skin) over the bowl.
3. As you bend the fruit, the seeds will ease themselves away from the skin and pithy membrane and, with a little help

from your fingers, should fall neatly and cleanly into the bowl.
4. Add the liqueur, cover and refrigerate at least 1 hour or until thoroughly chilled. Before serving, spoon into 4 glasses or dishes and garnish each with a sprig of watercress.

Parma Ham with Fresh Figs   *Serves 4*

A wonderful, fragrant combination which is one of my autumnal treats whenever I am in the region of Parma.

8oz (225g) Parma ham, very thinly sliced
12 to 16 fresh figs

1. Cover 4 plates with the ham.
2. Gently wash and dry the figs and arrange 3 or 4 on each plate.
3. Serve with white bread and butter.

Parma Ham Salad   *Serves 4*

Less costly than the above, this salad makes a superb starter and combines the best of all worlds in one dish.

8 lettuce leaves, washed and dried
1 small honeydew melon
6oz (175g) Parma ham
4oz (125g) Bel Paese cheese, rind removed
3 tblsp French dressing
1oz (25g) pecan nuts or walnuts

41

1. Line 4 individual plates with lettuce. Remove seeds from melon then scoop flesh into bowl with a teaspoon or melon baller.
2. Cut Parma ham into large squares and cheese into narrow strips. Add to bowl of melon with French dressing.
3. Toss well then divide equally between the 4 plates. Top each with pecans or walnuts and serve with crusty rolls and butter.

Chilled Artichokes with Hot Ravigote Sauce

Serves 4

In the style of French haute cuisine, the chilled artichokes with a hot buttery sauce is a sumptuous combination and perfect for a special family meal or entertaining. Other artichoke variations follow.

4 large globe artichokes

Sauce
3oz (75g) unsalted butter
½ level tsp French mustard
½ level tsp caster sugar
1½ tblsp wine vinegar
2 tsp lemon juice
½ small onion, peeled and chopped
1 hard-boiled egg, shelled and chopped
2 slightly rounded tblsp capers, drained and chopped
1 rounded tblsp chopped parsley

1. To prepare artichokes, cut off stems then remove first 2 rows of leaves (those nearest to the stem) as they tend to be woody and tough.
2. Cut tips of all the leaves with kitchen scissors then place artichokes, nose sides down, into a bowl of salted water. Leave to soak for ½ hour. Lift out, rinse and shake dry.

3. For cooking, stand the artichokes upright (this time noses uppermost) in a *large* saucepan to form a single layer. Add about 2 ins (5cm) water to pan plus 1½ level teaspoons salt.

4. Bring to boil, reduce heat and cover pan. Simmer about 45 minutes or until any of the leaves along the lower edge (near the stalk end) pull out easily. If they resist and appear tough, continue to cook for another 10 minutes or so.

5. Lift out of pan and put to drain upside down in a colander. Leave until cold then refrigerate a minimum of 2 to 3 hours.

6. Make sauce just before serving. Heat butter until sizzling in a pan then stir in all remaining ingredients. Warm through quickly, stirring. Pour into bowl. Add spoon.

7. Put artichokes on to individual plates. Pass the hot sauce separately, keeping it warm in between times.

Note

To tackle artichokes, use your fingers. Pick off each leaf, dip the pale and fleshy part into sauce and pass between teeth. Repeat until all the leaves have been dealt with, piling them up neatly on a separate plate. You should then find a core of leaves. Pull off and discard, then smartly lift out the furry choke bit by bit. Rinse your fingers in a finger bowl of water and slice of lemon. Lavish sauce on the heart (a flattish base) and eat with a knife and fork.

Hot Artichokes with Pepper and Garlic Butter

Serves 4

Prepare artichokes as directed in recipe above. Drain and serve straight away with a hot sauce made by melting 4oz (125g) butter and adding to it 1 peeled and crushed garlic clove and 1 rounded tablespoon Madagascan green peppers (Poivre Vert).

Cold Artichokes with Zesty Tomato Sauce

Serves 4

Prepare artichokes as given in first recipe and leave until cold. To prepare sauce, mix 4 rounded tablespoons thick mayonnaise with 2 teaspoons lemon juice, 2 teaspoons Worcestershire sauce, 1 peeled and crushed garlic clove, 1 level tablespoon tubed or canned tomato purée, ¼ teaspoon Tabasco and 1 level teaspoon basil.

Artichokes Vinaigrette

Serves 4

Prepare artichokes as given in first recipe and leave until cold. Serve each coated with 2 tablespoons homemade or bottled French dressing.

Grapefruit Cordon Pink

Serves 4

An off-beat starter cocktail with its own note of distinction — and luxury!

8 crisp lettuce leaves, washed and shredded
2 large pink grapefruit
1 large avocado pear
1 tblsp lemon juice
6oz (175g) smoked salmon, cut into strips
1 carton (¼pt or 150ml) whipping cream
½ level tsp salt
1 level tsp paprika
1 washed tomato, dried and cut into wedges

1. Put equal amounts of lettuce into 4 wine-type glasses on stems.
2. Peel grapefruit, removing all traces of pith. Holding each over a bowl to catch the juice, cut out segments of flesh in between the membranes with a sharp knife.
3. Peel avocado as you would peel a pear, starting from the pointed end. Halve and remove stone. Cut avocado into small dice. Add to bowl of grapefruit with half the lemon juice.
4. Gently stir in smoked salmon strips. To make sauce, whip cream until thick. Stir in salt with rest of lemon juice and paprika.
5. Add to grapefruit mixture. Toss well to mix. Spoon into glasses on top of lettuce. Garnish each with tomato wedges.

Palm Heart and Cashew Cocktail *Serves 4*

Light and unusual with a breath of exotica from the hearts of palm.

8 large lettuce leaves, washed and dried
1 can (about 15oz or 425g) hearts of palm (which look like leeks)
2oz (50g) salted cashews
1 garlic clove, peeled and crushed
2 rounded tblsp mayonnaise
1 rounded tblsp chopped fresh dill or parsley for garnishing

1. Arrange lettuce leaves over 4 bread and butter plates.
2. Drain palm hearts and cut into ½ in (1¼cm) thick slices. Put into mixing bowl.
3. Add cashews, garlic and mayonnaise. Pile equal amounts on to plates and sprinkle with dill or parsley. Serve with brown rolls and butter.

Thousand Island Celeriac Cocktail

Serves 4

Celeriac, which looks like a giant potato and with its subtle taste of celery, makes a tasty starter for almost any occasion.

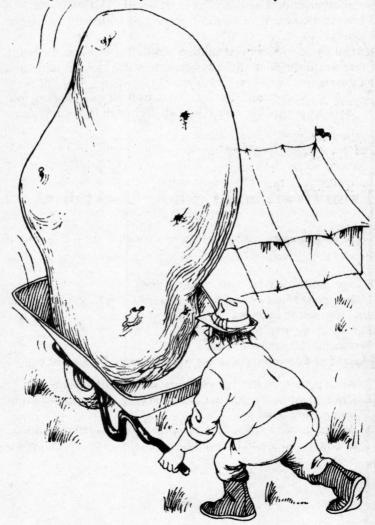

1½lb (675g) celeriac
cold water
1 to 1½ level tsp salt
1 tblsp lemon juice
¼pt (150ml) thick mayonnaise
1 Grade 3 egg, hard-boiled and chopped or grated
⅛ tsp cayenne pepper (very fiery)
3 level tblsp tomato ketchup
2 level tblsp stuffed olives, finely chopped
1 small onion, peeled and finely grated
1 level tblsp finely-chopped parsley
4 extra stuffed olives for garnishing

1. Peel celeriac thickly (flesh immediately underneath skin is hard), cut into slices then cut slices into strips about double the thickness of matchsticks.
2. Put into large pan, cover with cold water then add salt and lemon juice. Bring to boil, lower heat and cover.
3. Simmer about 15 minutes or until just tender. Drain. Leave until completely cold in covered bowl.
4. To make Thousand Island dressing, beat mayonnaise with egg, cayenne pepper, tomato ketchup, chopped olives, grated onion and parsley.
5. Add to celeriac and toss. Pile into 4 bowls and decorate each with an olive.

Hot Celeriac Cocktail *Serves 4*

Prepare celeriac and cook as above. Drain thoroughly. Return to pan. Add 3oz (75g) chopped and crisply-fried bacon, 1 small grated onion and 5 tablespoons French dressing. Toss. Spoon on to 4 plates and sprinkle with grated carrot. Serve while still hot.

Crab Cocktail

Serves 4

A close relation to Britain's favourite starter, Prawn Cocktail, this version is even better and simply made with a can of Queen crab and cocktail sauce.

½ medium round lettuce, washed and dried
6 rounded tblsp thick mayonnaise
2 rounded tblsp tomato ketchup
½ tsp Worcestershire sauce
½ tsp creamed horseradish sauce
2 to 3 level tsp lemon juice
1 can (about 7oz or 200g) Queen crab, drained and flaked
paprika
4 unpeeled prawns for garnish

1. Shred lettuce with a stainless knife and divide equally between 4 glasses. Leave aside temporarily.
2. Gently whisk together the mayonnaise with ketchup, Worcestershire and horseradish sauces and the lemon juice.
3. Combine with crabmeat and, when all the flakes are thoroughly coated with sauce, spoon into glasses.
4. Sprinkle each with paprika then decorate with a whole prawn. Serve with brown bread and butter.

Rosolli

Serves 4

Rosolli belongs to Finland where it is topped with soured cream, eaten with dark bread and thick butter, and swished down with tots of vodka.

4oz (125g) pickled beetroot, drained weight if from a bought jar
4oz (125g) cold cooked potatoes

4oz (125g) cold cooked carrots
4oz (125g) Polish-style gherkins (rather like pickled cucumbers)
4oz (125g) Golden Delicious or Cox apples
1 small onion, peeled and grated
2 tblsp French dressing
4oz (125g) cold cooked chicken, tongue or garlic sausage, cut
   into strips
1 carton (5oz or 142ml) soured cream

1. Dice beetroot, potatoes, carrots, gherkins and peeled apples.
   Put into a mixing bowl.
2. Add onions, dressing and either chicken, tongue or garlic
   sausage. Toss well to mix.
3. Put on to 4 plates and top each generously with soured
   cream. Serve with wholemeal bread and butter, or rye bread
   if preferred.

Taramosalata   *Serves 8*

If you dismiss this as just another version of a Greek classic,
please come back and give it a try. It is different from usual in
that the base is potatoes instead of breadcrumbs and the texture
is as smooth as cream. The flavour is also superb and, as usual,
Taramosalata is best scooped up with warm Pitta bread, now
available from many supermarket chains in addition to
Mediterranean and Eastern grocery stores.

6oz (175g) freshly-boiled potatoes (cooked weight)
2 tblsp boiling water
2 tblsp lemon juice
1 tblsp wine vinegar
4oz (125g) smoked cod's roe (available in pots)
4 tblsp olive oil
1 garlic clove, peeled and sliced
pepper to taste

1. Mash potatoes, then put into blender goblet or food processor with water, lemon juice, vinegar, cod's roe, oil and garlic.
2. Run machine until mixture forms a smooth purée then tip out into a mixing bowl. Beat in pepper.
3. Transfer to either 8 plates or to a small serving bowl with spoon. Serve with the warm Pitta bread.

Tip

Sometimes the roe is available by the piece from Jewish delicatessens or fishmongers, but do remember that you must allow for the weight of the skin so I suggest you buy at least double the amount in the recipe.

Cheese-Dressed Tomatoes   *Serves 4*

For those who grow their own or who are able to take advantage of gluts when they appear in the market place, this is a reasonably quick-to-prepare tomato starter with a certain touch of American flair.

1½lb (675g) ripe tomatoes, blanched and skinned
1 large Spanish-type onion, peeled
6oz (175g) cream cheese
4 tblsp single cream
salt and pepper to taste
4 level tblsp chopped parsley

1. Slice tomatoes thinly and use to cover 4 bread and butter plates.
2. Thinly slice onions and separate slices into rings. Arrange on top of tomatoes.
3. Beat cream cheese with cream and season to taste with salt and pepper. If too thick to pour like mayonnaise, thin down with a little milk.
4. Spoon over tomatoes and sprinkle with parsley. Serve with crusty French bread and butter.

Tomatoes Provençale

Serves 4

Prepare tomatoes exactly as above. Put on to 4 plates and coat with 6 tablespoons French dressing to which has been added 2 peeled and crushed garlic cloves and 3 heaped tablespoons chopped parsley.

Kiss of Paradise

Serves 4 to 6

I 'invented' this once when I inherited a box of red peppers and some friends simultaneously came to see us armed with a tray of farm eggs. It's flavoursome and appetising and is suitable both for summer and winter.

6 large red peppers
boiling water
8oz (225g) onions, peeled and coarsely grated
6 Grade 1 or 2 hard-boiled eggs
6 tblsp French dressing
salt and pepper to taste
black olives

1. Cut tops off peppers, remove inside seeds and discard. Put peppers into large pan.
2. Cover with boiling water and top with lid. Boil steadily for 10 minutes. Drain, rinse and leave in colander until completely cold.
3. Cut peppers into thin strips and put into mixing bowl. Add onions. Grate eggs directly over the top.
4. Pour over dressing and toss lightly. Season to taste with salt and pepper.
5. Mound on to 4 or 6 plates and stud with olives.

Note
If liked, line plates with lettuce leaves.

Ham Baked Avocados

Serves 4

Hot avocados are an unusual treat and this recipe happens to be an old favourite and always well received by family and friends. If serving 8, just double all the ingredients.

crumbs from 3 large slices fresh white bread, including crusts
2oz (50g) Polish-style sweet-sour gherkins, chopped
2oz (50g) salted cashews, coarsely chopped
4oz (125g) lean ham, cut into strips
2oz (50g) onion, peeled and grated
1oz (25g) butter or margarine, melted
1 tblsp double cream or undiluted evaporated milk
salt and pepper to taste
2 large, ripe avocados
1½ to 2 tblsp lemon juice

Coating
4 level tblsp crushed potato crisps
2 medium tomatoes, sliced
1oz (25g) butter or margarine, melted

1. Mix crumbs with gherkins, cashews, ham, onion, butter or margarine and the cream or evaporated milk. Season to taste.
2. Halve avocados and remove stones. Scoop flesh into bowl, leaving avocado skins with ¼ in (just under 1cm) thick 'walls' in order to support the filling.
3. Mash the avocados with lemon juice then combine with breadcrumb mixture. Pile smoothly into avocado shells then sprinkle with potato crisps.
4. Top each half with slices of tomato then sprinkle with butter or margarine. Bake 8 minutes in oven set to 230°C (450°F), Gas 8. Serve straight away.

Cheese-Stuffed Tomatoes

Serves 4

A tasty starter appreciated by vegetarians — and others. If preferred, use 4 very large tomatoes instead of 8 medium.

8 medium tomatoes (about 1 to 1¼lb or 450 to 575g)
3oz (75g) mild Cheddar cheese, finely grated
2oz (50g) fresh white breadcrumbs
2oz (50g) onion, peeled and grated
1 level tblsp very finely-chopped parsley
½ level tsp prepared English mustard
salt to taste
1oz (25g) butter

1. Wash, dry and stalk tomatoes. Cut off tops at stalk ends and keep on one side.
2. Carefully scoop insides into a mixing bowl with a teaspoon, taking care not to puncture tomato cups. Remove tough cores from pulp with your fingers and discard. Cut a thin sliver off the base of each tomato so that it stands upright without falling over.
3. For filling, stir cheese into tomato pulp followed by crumbs, onion, parsley, mustard and salt to taste. Mix thoroughly.
4. Spoon equal amounts into tomato cups and stand on a greased baking tray. Dot with flakes of butter then add tops which were put aside.
5. Reheat 10 to 12 minutes near top of oven set to 220°C (425°F), Gas 7. Allow 2 per person and serve hot.

Felafel

Serves about 6 to 8

No visit to Israel is complete without a 'street-meal' of Felafel: crusty chick pea balls tucked into Pitta bread (a whole one each) interspersed with salad and a drizzle of dressing — Tahina or mayonnaise. My way of serving these savouries over here is to offer them round — either hot or cold — with a dip of Tahina (sesame seed paste).

3 rounded tblsp burghul or cracked wheat, available from health food shops, delicatessens, oriental grocers and some super-market chains
6 tblsp boiling water
8oz (225g) chick peas, soaked overnight in plenty of water
1 garlic clove, peeled and sliced
2oz (50g) onion, peeled and coarsely chopped
1 rounded tblsp coarsely-chopped parsley
1 level tsp cumin seeds (optional)
2 level tblsp plain flour
1½ to 2 level tsp salt
¼ level tsp white pepper
oil for frying

1. Tip burghul or cracked wheat into a mixing bowl. Stir in the boiling water and leave to stand ½ hour.
2. Drain chick peas and leave uncooked. Tip into blender goblet or food processor and add garlic, onion and parsley. Grind coarsely.
3. Spoon into burghul then mix in cumin seeds, flour with salt to taste and pepper. When evenly combined, shape into 30 balls with damp hands.
4. Lower, a few at a time, into a deepish pan containing hot oil and fry 5 to 6 minutes or until golden brown and crisp.
5. Drain on paper towels, put cocktail sticks into each and arrange on a d'oyley-lined plate. Serve the Tahina in a separate dish.

Monkfish Goujons with Orange Sauce

Serves 4 to 6

Monkfish has, by virtue of price, become a delicacy, so keep this starter for special occasions. For those unfamiliar with Monkfish, it tastes very much like scampi and, when coated and fried, it is almost impossible to tell the difference. It is especially good served piping hot with a cool and spicy soured cream sauce flavoured with orange.

1½lb (675g) monkfish
salt
4 level tblsp self-raising flour
2 Grade 3 eggs, well beaten
oil in deep pan for frying

Sauce
 1 carton (5oz or 142ml) soured cream
1 level tsp finely-grated orange peel
½ level tsp ground ginger
⅛ level tsp nutmeg
1 tblsp orange juice
½ tblsp lemon juice
1 level tsp salt

1. Wash and dry monkfish and cut into strips about 2 in by ½ in (5cm by 1¼cm). Sprinkle with salt.
2. Coat with flour then dip each piece into the beaten eggs. Lower, a few pieces at a time, into deep pan of hot oil. Fry until deep gold, puffy and crisp; about 5 to 7 minutes.
3. Lift out of pan with a draining spoon and tip on to a plate covered with crumpled kitchen paper. Do not cover but keep hot.
4. For sauce, beat all ingredients well together and spoon into a bowl. To serve, put fried Goujons on to individual plates and accompany with the sauce.

Salmon and Mushroom Bowls on Almond Rice

Serves 4

An extravaganza of a fish dish which looks both attractive and elegant served in individual bowls.

6oz (175g) easy-cook long grain rice
½ level tsp salt
2oz (50g) flaked almonds
2½oz (62g) butter or margarine
2oz (50g) washed and dried button mushrooms, trimmed and sliced
1oz (25g) flour
½pt (275ml) warm milk
½ level tsp salt
1 medium can (about 7oz or 200g) pink salmon, drained and flaked
4oz (125g) Cheddar cheese, grated

1. Put rice in a pan with salt. Add 12 fluid oz (375ml) boiling water. Bring to boil and stir. Cover. Cook over medium heat for about 20 minutes or until rice grains are tender and have absorbed all the moisture.
2. Meanwhile fry almonds until pale gold in 1oz (25g) butter. Fork into rice and keep hot.
3. To make mushroom sauce, heat rest of butter until sizzling in a saucepan. Add mushrooms and fry gently for 3 minutes, turning.
4. Stir in flour then gradually blend in warm milk. Cook, stirring, until sauce comes to the boil and thickens. Add salt and salmon. Mix well and spoon over almond rice.
5. Sprinkle with cheese and brown under a hot grill. Serve straight away.

Tip
Tuna may be used instead of salmon.

Gnocchi Romana

Serves 6 to 8

A classic from Italy, easy to put together and a pleasure to eat. I like it on its own, piping hot from the oven, but it can be served with creamed spinach or baked tomato halves for variety.

1pt (575ml) milk
5oz (150g) semolina or polenta
1 level tsp salt
white pepper to taste
3oz (75g) butter
3oz (75g) grated Parmesan cheese
¼ level tsp ground nutmeg
1 Grade 2 egg, well-beaten

1. Pour milk into a pan and add semolina or polenta and salt. Bring to boil, stirring continuously.
2. Mix in the pepper and 2oz (50g) butter. Continue to cook gently until mixture becomes very thick. Stir all the time to prevent sticking and allow about 7 minutes over low heat.
3. Remove from heat and beat in 2oz (50g) Parmesan cheese, the nutmeg and beaten egg. Return to heat and bring just up to the boil.
4. Spread mixture, with wet knife, into a 12 by 8 in (30 by 22½cm) buttered Swiss roll tin. Cool to lukewarm then cover with a piece of greaseproof paper. Leave in the refrigerator until firm; about 2 to 3 hours.
5. To complete, cut into 1½ in (just under 4cm) squares and layer into a shallow, buttered heatproof dish. Go no higher than 3 layers.
6. Melt remaining butter and pour over the top. Sprinkle with last 1oz (25g) Parmesan cheese and reheat and brown for 20 minutes in oven set to 220°C (425°F), Gas 7.
7. Spoon out of dish and serve straight away.

Mushroom Crackle

Serves 4

A carefree starter made from reasonably-priced ingredients and a good beginning to a light meal.

1oz (25g) butter or margarine
1oz (25g) flour
½pt (275ml) milk
⅛ tsp dried thyme
6oz (175g) trimmed mushrooms, sliced
4oz (125g) Edam cheese, grated
salt and pepper to taste

Topping
3 large slices brown bread, cut into small dice
1oz (25g) butter or margarine, melted
2oz (50g) Edam cheese, grated
parsley sprigs

1. Melt butter or margarine in a pan. Stir in flour to form a roux.
2. Gradually blend in milk. Cook, stirring, until sauce comes to the boil and thickens. Stir in thyme and mushrooms and simmer gently, uncovered, for 5 minutes.
3. Stir occasionally then add cheese. Remove from heat and stir until melted. Season to taste.
4. Divide mixture equally between 4 well-buttered and individual ovenproof dishes.
5. Sprinkle with bread dice, trickle butter or margarine over the top followed by cheese. Brown under a hot grill then garnish each with a sprig of parsley.

Tunisian Baked Eggs

Serves 4

A flavourful and vivacious starter from Tunisia which is less complex to make than many other North African specialities.

3 tsp olive oil
1oz (25g) butter
12oz (350g) blanched tomatoes, skinned and chopped
1 medium washed and dried green pepper, de-seeded and cut
   into strips
1 rounded tblsp tubed or canned tomato purée
1 garlic clove, peeled
½ level tsp salt
4 Grade 3 eggs

1. Heat oil and butter in heavy-based frying pan. Add tomatoes, pepper strips and purée.
2. Crush garlic directly over the top. Mix in well then cook over a low heat for ¼ hour. Cover pan with lid or inverted enamel plate.
3. Uncover. Mix in salt. Continue to cook, stirring often, another 15 to 25 minutes or until tomato mixture is thick. Do not cover.
4. Break eggs, individually, over top of tomato mixture. Cover again. Cook gently about 10 to 15 minutes or until egg yolks are firm.
5. Spoon on to individual plates and serve with white bread.

Strawberry and Cheese Cocktail   *Serves 4*

An unlikely combination of ingredients at first sight, but one which works with great success.

6oz (175g) Edam cheese
4oz (125g) strawberries
4oz (125g) peeled prawns
½ medium cucumber, diced
4 tblsp dry white wine
sprigs of fresh mint for garnishing

1. Cut the cheese into ½ in (1cm) cubes. Wash and hull the strawberries and quarter.
2. In a large mixing bowl, mix together cheese, strawberries, prawns and cucumber.
3. Add the wine, toss lightly then cover and chill for 45 minutes in the refrigerator.
4. Divide the salad between 4 individual serving dishes, spooning over any leftover liquid. Garnish with mint and accompany with brown bread and butter.

Salad Niçoise

Serves 4

One of the tastiest exports from the Mediterranean, with a decorative look and happy temperament. It teams well with Anjou rosé wine or Mateus from Portugal.

½ round lettuce
12oz (350g) blanched and skinned tomatoes
8oz (225g) boiled new potatoes
8oz (225g) sliced green beans, cooked and left to get cold
5 tblsp French dressing, homemade or shop bought
1 can (7oz or 200g) tuna, drained and flaked
8 canned anchovy fillets in oil, drained
2 Grade 2 hard-boiled eggs, cut into wedges
12 black olives
1 level tblsp capers, well-drained

1. Wash and dry lettuce. Use to line base of shallow dish.
2. Cut tomatoes into wedges and potatoes into dice. Put both into mixing bowl. Toss gently with beans and half the French dressing.
3. Spoon into dish over lettuce then coat with rest of dressing.
4. Stud with flakes of tuna then garnish with a criss-cross of anchovies, the eggs, olives and capers. Serve with crusty French bread or rolls.

Peperonata Pasta

Serves at least 8

Peperonata is like Bolognese sauce without the meat and makes a fine contribution to plates of spaghetti. It is full of character and colour and best made in summer when the ingredients are at their most prolific.

2lb (900g) bright red peppers
1lb (450g) onions
2 garlic cloves
2lb (900g) bright red, ripe tomatoes, blanched and skinned
5 tblsp salad oil
2 to 3 level tsp salt
pepper to taste
freshly-cooked spaghetti, allowing 2 to 3oz (50 to 75g) raw
   weight per person

1. Wash and dry peppers then cut in half and remove inside fibres and seeds. Cut flesh into narrow strips.
2. Peel onions and thinly slice. Repeat with cloves of garlic. Cut tomatoes into wedges.
3. Put peppers, onions, garlic and tomatoes into a heavyish pan with oil, salt and pepper. Stir well to mix.
4. Bring to a gentle boil, stirring constantly. Cover and simmer very gently for 1 hour. Uncover.
5. Continue to cook over a minimal heat for another 20 to 30 minutes or until most of the liquid in the pan has evaporated and the mixture is thick. It is essential to stir often as anything containing tomatoes has a tendency to stick.
6. Toss drained spaghetti with 1oz (25g) butter or margarine or 1 tablespoon salad oil to give it a gloss. Transfer to 8 plates and top with Peperonata mixture. Sprinkle thickly with grated Parmesan cheese and serve straight away.

Bacon Peanut Rice

Serves 4 to 6

An unusual blend here, and useful if you are looking for something reasonably economical and a bit out-of-the-ordinary.

2oz (50g) butter or margarine
2 tsp salad oil
4oz (125g) streaky bacon, chopped
8oz (225g) easy-cook, long grain rice
1pt (575ml) chicken stock
1 heaped tblsp chopped parsley
2 well-rounded tblsp crunchy peanut butter
salt and pepper to taste

Topping
2 heaped tblsp salted peanuts, finely chopped
2 level tblsp Parmesan cheese, grated
1 level tsp finely-grated lemon peel

1. Heat butter or margarine and oil in pan until sizzling. Mix in streaky bacon and fry gently until soft.
2. Add rice and stock then bring to boil, stirring. Reduce heat to medium, cover pan and cook for 20 minutes or until rice grains are tender and have absorbed all the liquid.
3. Fork in parsley and peanut butter then season to taste with salt and pepper. Remove from heat and spoon on to warm plates.
4. Mix together the peanuts, cheese and lemon peel and sprinkle over each portion of rice. Serve very hot.

Mango Prawns

Serves 6

An unusually tasty sweet-sour prawn curry for a lightish starter which goes very well with freshly-cooked Basmati rice and natural yogurt mixed with golden-toasted coconut — about 1oz (25g) to every small carton of yogurt.

6oz (175g) cooking apples
8oz (225g) onions
2 tblsp salad oil (use a bland one such as corn or sunflower)
½ to 1 level tblsp mild curry powder
1 level tblsp flour
1 can (14oz or 400g) tomatoes
2 well-rounded tblsp mango chutney
¼ to ½ tsp cayenne pepper (remember, it is very fiery)
1lb (450g) peeled prawns
1 to 2 level tsp salt

1. Peel apples and cut into small cubes. Peel onions and grate finely.
2. Heat oil until sizzling then add apples and onions. Fry until pale gold. Stir in curry powder and flour. Cook 1 minute.
3. Add can of tomatoes, chutney and pepper. Crush whole tomatoes against sides of pan then stir mixture thoroughly to combine.
4. Bring to the boil and cover. Simmer 30 minutes. Add prawns and heat through briefly, allowing about 5 to 7 minutes but no longer as the fish might toughen.
5. Season curry with salt then spoon on to plates already lined with hot rice. Serve with the accompaniments suggested above, plus dishes of thinly-sliced onions and cut-up bananas sprinkled with lemon juice to prevent browning.

Banana and Ham Gratin

Serves 4

A substantial starter with a blissful flavour.

1 medium banana
4 thin slices of ham

Sauce
½oz (15g) Dutch unsalted butter
½oz (15g) plain flour
½pt (275ml) milk
1 tsp lemon juice
½ level tsp French mustard
3oz (75g) Gouda cheese, grated
salt and pepper to taste
chopped parsley for garnishing

1. Halve banana then cut each half lengthwise to give 4 pieces. Wrap each piece in a slice of ham and place in individual heatproof serving dishes, first well-buttered.
2. To make sauce, place butter, flour and milk into a pan and whisk over a gentle heat until smooth and slightly thickened. Continue cooking, stirring continuously, for 2 minutes.
3. Remove from heat. Whisk in lemon juice and mustard. Stir in cheese then season to taste with salt and pepper. Pour over banana and ham wraps.
4. Grill until golden brown then sprinkle each with chopped parsley.

Asparagus Appetisers   *Serves 4*

Deliciously light and appetising and just the thing to preface a full meal.

4 medium thick slices of brown bread
4oz (125g) Gouda cheese, grated
1 can (7oz or 700g) asparagus tips, well-drained
freshly-milled black pepper

Garnish
paprika
2 stuffed olives, sliced

1. Cut bread into 4 by 3½ in (8¾cm) rounds and toast on one side only.
2. Sprinkle untoasted sides with 3oz (75g) of the cheese then arrange asparagus tips, in a fan shape, on top of each.
3. Sprinkle with remaining cheese then brown under a hot grill. Dust with paprika then garnish with slices of olives. Serve hot.

Crunchy Lettuce Cups
Serves 4

Crisp and crunchy and just the thing to set the appetite tingling!

4oz (125g) Edam cheese
1 small celery stalk
2 green dessert apples, unpeeled and cut into small dice
2 tblsp lemon juice
4 to 6 radishes, thinly sliced
1oz (25g) walnuts, coarsely chopped
4 crisp lettuce leaves
4 to 6 tblsp yogurt salad dressing
scissor-snipped chives for garnishing

1. Cut cheese and celery into 1 in (2½cm) long matchsticks.
2. Put apples into a large bowl, sprinkle with lemon juice and mix well. Stir in cheese, celery, radishes and walnuts.
3. Put lettuce leaves on to individual plates and top with cheese mixture.
4. Coat with dressing and sprinkle with chives. Serve with crusty white rolls and butter.

Main Courses

OK — so your main courses are nothing to boast about: your stews are insipid, your chicken stringy, your repertoire uninspired. What you need are some new ideas to liven up meals for the family and to impress your guests. Look no further — here is a selection of delicious, exciting, *different* recipes for main meals, with meat, fish and poultry, and vegetarian, which will transform your cookery reputation and ensure that, never again, will you say, 'I can't cook main courses.'

Salmon Gratin à la Crème *Serves 4 generously*

Lovely for family eating and just as good for entertaining — all you do for eight servings is to double the ingredients.

5oz (150g) easy-cook long grain rice
½pt (150ml) boiling water
½ level tsp salt
3oz (75g) butter or margarine
1½oz (40g) flour
½pt (275ml) milk
juice of 1 medium lemon, strained
1 can (7oz or 200g) red salmon
1 level tsp tarragon
salt and pepper to taste

Topping
2oz (50g) Cheddar cheese, finely grated
1oz (25g) lightly-toasted breadcrumbs
1oz (25g) butter or margarine, melted

1. Cook rice in boiling water and salt for 20 minutes or until grains are plump and tender and have absorbed all the liquid. Stir as rice comes to the boil then cover and leave undisturbed until cooking time is completed.
2. Fork in half the butter or margarine and keep hot. For sauce, melt rest of butter or margarine in saucepan. Stir in flour to make roux.
3. Cook 1 minute without browning then gradually blend in milk. Bring to boil, stirring continually until thickened. Mix in lemon juice.
4. Flake salmon, discarding skin and bones. Add to sauce mixture with its liquor. Add tarragon then season to taste. Keep hot.
5. Divide rice between 4 individual heatproof dishes, first well butttered. Make slight dip in centres then fill with salmon

mixture.

6. Sprinkle evenly with cheese, crumbs and melted butter or margarine then brown under a hot grill. Serve with mange tout or spinach and baby carrots tossed in butter and a trace of nutmeg.

Seafood Crêpes with Watercress

Serves 4

I have used smoked cod and no shellfish in one of my favourite dishes, and enlivened the filling with chopped watercress.

Pancake Batter
4oz (125g) plain flour
1 level tsp powder mustard
tip of the knife amount of grated nutmeg
1 Grade 3 egg
½pt (275ml) cold milk
1 tsp salad oil or melted butter (use margarine if preferred)
white cooking fat for greasing, melted

Filling
1oz (25g) butter or margarine
1oz (25g) plain flour
¼pt (150ml) white wine
1 carton (5oz or 142ml) soured cream
3 level tblsp homemade or best quality shop-bought mayonnaise
1lb (450g) smoked cod fillet, cooked and flaked
seasoning to taste
1 bunch watercress, leaves washed, dried and chopped

Topping
¼pt (150ml) single cream
2 tblsp mayonnaise as above
4oz (125g) mild Cheddar cheese, finely grated

1. To make batter, sift flour with mustard and nutmeg into a mixing bowl.
2. Make a well in the centre. Drop in egg then, beating all the time, mix to a thick and creamy batter with half the milk.
3. Stir in rest of milk with either the salad oil or the butter or margarine. Cover. Refrigerate 1 to 2 hours.
4. To make pancakes, brush an 8 ins (20cm), heavy-based and smooth pan with melted white cooking fat. Heat until hot, but not smoking, and pour off any surplus as this could cause pancakes to stick.
5. Stir batter then pour in enough to cover base of pan fairly thinly; about 3 tablespoons. Cook until underside is golden then turn or toss over and cook until second side is also golden and speckled with brown spots.
6. Remove from pan straight on to a clean tea towel. Repeat, using all the pancake mixture and making a total of 8 pancakes. Leave on one side temporarily.
7. To make filling, melt butter in a clean saucepan. Mix in flour to form a roux. Cook 1 minute over a low heat, stirring continuously.
8. Gradually blend in white wine. Cook, still stirring, until mixture just comes up to the boil and thickens. Add soured cream, mayonnaise and the flaked smoked cod.
9. Heat through 7 minutes or until very hot. Stir often to prevent sticking. Season to taste. Add chopped watercress.
10. Put equal amounts on to pancakes and roll up. Place in well-buttered, oblong heatproof dish, making sure joins are underneath and pancakes form a single layer.
11. Beat topping ingredients well together then spoon over pancakes. Reheat 12 to 15 minutes near top of oven set to 220°C (425°F), Gas 7. When ready, the cheese should just be melting and turning brown.
12. Remove from oven and transfer to 4 warm plates. Garnish each with a sprig of crisp watercress but otherwise leave unaccompanied as crêpes are rich and sustaining.

Finnan Potatoes

Serves 4

When those lovely, large winter potatoes are readily available, why not bake them in their jackets and then lavish them with cream, smoked or Finnan haddock (depending on which part of the country you come from) and cheese? They make a treat of a meal served with crisply cooked cabbage and fried or baked mushrooms.

4 large potatoes (about 2lb or 900g)
salad oil
2oz (50g) butter or margarine
4 tblsp double cream
12oz (350g) smoked haddock fillet (Finnan haddock), cooked and flaked
3 level tblsp chopped parsley
salt and pepper to taste
1 level tsp prepared English mustard
3oz (75g) Double Gloucester cheese, grated

1. Wash, scrub and dry potatoes then prick all over with a fork. Put on to a greased baking tray then brush potatoes with oil to keep skins shiny and pliable.
2. Bake 1½ to 2 hours in oven centre set to 190°C (375°F), Gas 5. Remove from oven and cut in halves lengthwise.
3. When cool enough to handle, spoon insides into a bowl and mash very finely. Beat in butter or margarine, cream, haddock and parsley.
4. Season to taste with salt and pepper, stir in mustard then pile mixture back into potato shells.
5. Sprinkle with cheese then reheat and brown near top of oven set to 220°C (425°F), Gas 7. Allow 15 to 20 minutes then serve straight away.

Baltimore Crab Cakes

Serves 4

A magnificent contribution from America's Eastern seaboard are these sizzling Crab Cakes which, in their country of origin, are made exclusively from fresh crabs, locally caught. Serve them as an off-beat main course with shredded lettuce and finely sliced cucumber tossed in French dressing and, in the absence of fresh crab, use frozen or canned.

2 cans (each 7oz or 200g) Queen crab or the same weight in fresh or frozen crabmeat, thawed
3oz (75g) fresh brown breadcrumbs
2 Grade 3 eggs, beaten
1 level tblsp parsley, very finely chopped
1 tsp Worcestershire sauce
1 level tsp salt
1 level tsp American mustard
1 rounded tblsp thick mayonnaise based on eggs (and *not* salad cream)
3 to 4 tblsp salad oil for frying

1. Shred crabmeat with 2 forks and put into mixing bowl.
2. Gently fork in crumbs, eggs, parsley, Worcestershire sauce, salt, mustard and mayonnaise.
3. Leave mixture to stand for 15 minutes so that the crumbs have time to absorb moisture and any surplus can then be left behind.
4. Shape into 4 large cakes and fry fairly briskly in hot oil, allowing 5 minutes per side. Drain on crumpled kitchen paper and serve straight away, while still very hot.

Bouillabaisse with Rouille

Serves 4

A flamboyant fish bouquet from Southern France, Bouillabaisse is a full-blown soup-cum-stew, extravagantly scented with saffron and served with a hot chili sauce — which you prepare yourself — called Rouille. It is best to make the sauce first.

Rouille

1 large washed green pepper, de-seeded and chopped
1 small washed green chili, slit and de-seeded then chopped
¼pt (150ml) plus 4 extra tblsp water
2 pickled red peppers (obtainable in jars), very finely chopped
3 garlic cloves, peeled and crushed
5 rounded tblsp fresh white breadcrumbs
1 level tsp salt
6 tblsp olive oil

Bouillabaisse

12oz (350g) onions, peeled
4 tblsp olive oil
3 cans (each 14oz or 200g) tomatoes
3 garlic cloves, peeled and crushed
2 bouquet garni bags
1 large bayleaf
½ level tsp saffron strands
1pt (575ml) dry white wine
2½pt (1½ litres) water
1lb (450g) fish trimmings
1½lb (675g) plaice or sole fillet, diced
12oz (350g) peeled prawns
2lb (900g) fresh mussels, thoroughly scrubbed under cold water

1. To make Rouille, cook green pepper and chili in the water for about 10 to 15 minutes. Keep pan covered and heat low.
2. Drain thoroughly. Add pickled peppers, garlic, crumbs and salt. Beat in olive oil. Leave aside for time being.
3. For Bouillabaisse, thinly slice onions. Put into large pan with oil and fry very gently for 15 minutes or until soft and still pale gold. Add next 8 ingredients. Bring to boil, stirring. Cover.
4. Lower heat and simmer very gently for 1½ hours. Remove bouquet garni bags. Rub through fine mesh sieve into clean pan. Bring to boil. Add 3 tablespoons to the Rouille. Add plaice to pan. Simmer 5 minutes.

5. Mix in prawns and mussels. Simmer gently another 5 minutes. Ladle into bowls. Serve with slices of French bread and pass the Rouille separately, to be added as a condiment.

Salmon Doria with Tarragon Sauce

Serves 4

An attractive combination of flavours makes this a luxury dish in the grand style.

½ medium cucumber, peeled
4 salmon steaks, each 6oz or 175g (thawed if frozen)
2oz (50g) butter or margarine
1oz (25g) flour
½pt (275ml) milk
½ level tsp dried tarragon or 1 level tblsp fresh, finely chopped
salt and pepper to taste
6oz (225g) American long grain rice cooked as directed on packet in ¾pt (425ml) water with 1½ level tsp salt
4 lemon wedges for garnishing

1. Slit cucumber lengthwise into 4 strips. Remove seeds and discard. Chop flesh and tip into pan. Cover with boiling water for 5 minutes. Drain and leave aside.
2. Poach salmon, uncovered, for 10 minutes in a large, shallow pan with just enough salted water to cover.
3. Meanwhile, make sauce. Melt 1oz (25g) butter or margarine in pan and stir in flour to form a roux. Cook 1 minute.
4. Gradually blend in milk. Cook, stirring, until sauce bubbles and thickens. Stir in tarragon and cucumber then season to taste with salt and pepper.
5. Fork rest of butter into cooked rice and arrange on 4 dinner plates. Drain salmon and place on top. Coat with sauce then garnish each with a lemon wedge. Serve straight away.

Oven-Fried Mackerel Crisps   *Serves 4*

Nothing can beat fresh mackerel for flavour, and when blanketed in an unusual coating of packeted sage and onion stuffing, oven-fried in oil and garnished with wedges of orange, you partake of a noble experience!

4 medium mackerel, cleaned and boned (ask fishmonger to do this for you)
2 Grade 2 eggs
1 packet (3½oz or 99g) sage and onion stuffing
oil for oven-frying
1 small orange, cut into 4 wedges

1. Wash and dry mackerel. Beat eggs in a deepish enamel plate until foamy then add mackerel, one at a time, and coat completely.
2. Tip stuffing mix on to a piece of foil or greaseproof paper. Lift each mackerel, singly, on to stuffing and toss over and over until it is completely covered.
3. Leave to rest for 45 minutes to give coating time to settle and cling to the fish.
4. Meanwhile pour 1 in (2½cm) oil into a medium-sized roasting tin and heat 10 to 15 minutes just above oven centre set to 200°C (400°F), Gas 6.
5. Add mackerel, baste with hot oil and return to oven. Cook 25 to 30 minutes or until fish is tender. Serve with boiled potatoes and finely shredded Chinese leaves cooked quickly in a little milk with the addition of seasoning to taste and 2 cloves. Garnish fish with orange wedges.

Smoky Haddock on Nut Rice   *Serves 6*

A kind of savoury rice and nut pudding with smoked haddock
— a fish dish which could never be described as run-of-the-mill.

8oz (225g) easy-cook long grain rice
1pt (575ml) boiling water
1 level tsp salt
3oz (75g) butter or margarine
1oz (25g) walnuts, finely chopped
1 level tsp prepared mustard
1 garlic clove, peeled and crushed (optional)
1lb (450g) smoked haddock, cooked and flaked
2 Grade 3 eggs, beaten
2 slightly rounded tblsp lightly-toasted breadcrumbs

1. Put rice into saucepan with boiling water and salt. Stir round
   twice, cover and boil gently for 15 to 20 minutes or until rice
   grains are tender and have absorbed all the moisture.
2. Fork in 2oz (50g) butter or margarine, walnuts, mustard,
   garlic clove if used, haddock flakes and eggs.
3. Toss over and over gently with 2 spoons to mix, then spread
   evenly into an 8 ins (20cm) round ovenproof dish, first well-
   buttered.
4. Sprinkle with breadcrumbs then melt rest of butter and
   trickle over the top.
5. Leave uncovered. Reheat and brown 30 minutes just above
   oven centre set to 200°C (400°F), Gas 6. Serve straight away
   with a crunchy salad or cooked vegetables to taste.

Fish and Banana Exotica   *Serves 4*

Mildly curried and flavoured with banana and chutney, this is a
pleasing luxury fish dish to keep up your sleeve.

77

A fish dish to keep up your sleeve

6oz (175g) pasta shells
boiling salted water
1oz (25g) butter or margarine
2 level tsp mild curry powder
2oz (50g) onion, peeled and finely grated
1 level tsp *each* turmeric, paprika and garam masala (curry spices without fire!)
2 level tblsp fruit chutney
2 medium bananas
2 tblsp lemon juice
1lb (450g) plaice fillets
8oz (225g) natural yogurt
1 carton (5oz or 142ml) soured cream
extra paprika

1. Cook pasta shells as directed on the packet in boiling salted water, allowing no more than 10 minutes. Drain. Return to saucepan.
2. Stand over a low heat and toss in butter or margarine, curry powder, onion, the spices and chutney.
3. Spoon into fairly large, buttered heatproof dish. Slice bananas directly on top of pasta, then spread out to form an even layer. Sprinkle with lemon juice. Top with plaice fillets.
4. Beat yogurt and soured cream together then spoon over fish. Sprinkle with paprika and cook, uncovered, 25 to 30 minutes in oven set to 200°C (400°F), Gas 6. Serve with a mixed salad or baked tomato halves.

Prawn Pot-Pourri

Serves 4 to 6

A fanciful quickie for a small, intimate dinner party.

2oz (50g) butter or margarine
4 large washed and dried celery stalks, cut into very thin strips
12oz (350g) blanched tomatoes, skinned and cut into wedges
1 level tsp salt
1lb (450g) peeled prawns, thawed if frozen
6oz (150g) Cheddar cheese, grated
1 level tsp mixed herbs

1. Heat butter or margarine in pan. Add celery and fry very gently for 10 to 15 minutes or until just beginning to soften and turn light gold.
2. Remove from heat and stir in tomatoes and salt. Arrange over base of greased heatproof dish, shallow rather than deep.
3. Cover with prawns then sprinkle with cheese and herbs. Reheat 15 minutes near top of oven set to 220°C (425°F), Gas 7. Serve hot with whole baked mushrooms and boiled potatoes tossed in butter.

Sole Pot-Pourri

Serves 4 to 6

Make exactly as above but substitute 1lb (450g) lemon sole fillets, cut into thin strips, for the prawns. Cook 20 to 25 minutes just above oven centre set to 200°C (400°F), Gas 6.

Savoury Custard Pie

Serves 6 generously

Not quite a Quiche but closely related, here is a pie which takes well to lunch or supper, providing a tasty main course which is nourishing and reasonably economical.

6oz (175g) shortcrust pastry (made with 6oz or 175g flour and 3oz or 75g fat etc)
1oz (25g) butter or margarine
4oz (125g) onion, peeled and very thinly sliced
2oz (50g) fresh white breadcrumbs
¾pt (425ml) milk
3 Grade 2 eggs, well-beaten
1 level tsp salt
¼ level tsp white pepper
1oz (25g) Cheddar cheese, very finely grated
watercress for garnishing

1. Set oven to 190°C (375°F), Gas 5. Roll out pastry thinly and use to line an 8 ins (20cm) buttered pie plate with rim. Refrigerate temporarily.
2. Heat butter or margarine in a small frying pan. Add onion and fry fairly gently until golden. Cool. Use to cover base of pastry, pouring in left over butter as well.
3. For filling, put crumbs into a saucepan, add milk and heat until hot. Draw away from heat. Cool to lukewarm. Gradually beat in eggs.
4. Season to taste with salt and pepper then pour into pie crust. Sprinkle cheese on top and bake 45 to 50 minutes in oven centre.
5. Garnish with watercress and serve hot or cold with a crisp salad.

Macaroni Carbonara

Serves 4

One of those dishes you can make after a day's shopping or work with minimal effort and produce a sophisticated Italian classic in about half an hour.

12oz (350g) wide, bias cut macaroni, called Penne
4oz (125g) washed button mushrooms, trimmed and dried then
    thinly sliced
1oz (25g) butter or margarine
3oz (75g) Parma ham or British ham, chopped
2oz (50g) small black olives
3oz (75g) grated Parmesan cheese
¼pt (150ml) single cream ⎫
3 Grade 3 eggs   ⎭ beaten together
salt and pepper to taste
extra Parmesan cheese for sprinkling over the top

1. Cook macaroni in boiling salted water as directed on the
   packet. If no specific instructions are given, allow about 10
   to 12 minutes or until tender but not over-soft.
2. Drain and return to saucepan. Keep hot. Meanwhile, fry
   mushrooms quickly in the butter or margarine for 3 minutes.
3. Tip into macaroni. Add ham, olives, cheese and the beaten
   cream and eggs. Stand pan over minimal heat.
4. Toss with 2 spoons until egg mixture looks lightly scrambled
   and clings to macaroni. Pile on to 4 warm plates and sprinkle
   with extra cheese. Serve while hot and accompany with a
   crisp salad.

Blue Cheese Flan

Serves 4

A close relation to a Quiche, but somehow more elegant. I can
see this being a great success with all those who are devotees of
blue cheese.

shortcrust cheese pastry made with:
6oz (175g) plain flour
3oz (75g) mixture of butter and white cooking fat
2oz (50g) mature Cheddar cheese, very finely grated
about 2 to 2½ tblsp single cream to mix

82

Filling
6oz (175g) cream cheese
4 level tblsp scissor-snipped fresh chives or the same amount of
   green part of leek, very finely chopped
3oz (75g) blue cheese
2oz (50g) butter, softened but not melted
2 Grade 3 eggs
¼ level tsp white pepper
salt to taste

1. To make pastry, sift flour into a bowl then rub in fats finely.
   Toss in cheese. Mix to a stiff dough with cream. Knead
   lightly until smooth.
2. Wrap in clingfilm or foil and refrigerate 20 minutes. Turn
   out on to a floured surface and roll out fairly thinly. Use to
   line a buttered flan dish (metal or pottery) of about 8 ins
   (20cm) in diameter by 1 in (2½cm) in depth.
3. Line with foil to prevent pastry rising as it cooks, then bake
   20 minutes near top of oven set to 220°C (425°F), Gas 7.
4. Put all filling ingredients into blender goblet or food processor
   and run machine until smooth.
5. Remove flan case from oven, carefully lift out foil then pour
   in blue cheese filling.
6. Return to oven, this time set to 190°C (375°F), Gas 5.
   Continue to bake a further 30 minutes when filling should be
   golden brown and puffy. Cut into wedges and serve hot with
   salad.

Egg and Mushroom Cream Bake

Serves 4 to 5

Blissfully easy to put together and a pleasant change for those
who favour fishless and meatless dishes.

6 Grade 3 hard-boiled eggs
1lb (450g) cold cooked potatoes
1 can condensed cream of mushroom soup
2 tblsp boiling water
3 tblsp single cream
2 level tblsp lightly-toasted breadcrumbs
1oz (25g) butter or margarine, melted
paprika

1. Cut eggs and potatoes into slices
2. Put soup into a pan with water and cream. Heat, whisking gently all the time, until completely smooth.
3. Fill a 2½ pint (1½ litre) well-buttered, fairly shallow heatproof dish with half the potatoes, all the eggs and half the soup mixture.
4. Cover with rest of potatoes then coat with remaining soup mixture.
5. Sprinkle with crumbs, trickle butter or margarine on top then dust lightly with paprika.
6. Reheat and brown for 20 minutes near top of oven set to 220°C (425°F), Gas 7. Serve with a green salad.

Topsy-Turvy Tomato Pudding   *Serves 4*

A fun one, this, which is perfectly timed for midweek eating. A happy partner is a mixed salad tossed in French dressing.

1 can (about 14oz or 400g) tomatoes
1 level tsp marjoram
8oz (225g) self-raising flour
1 level tsp salt
1 level tsp powder mustard
4oz (125g) butter or margarine
4oz (125g) Dutch Gouda cheese, grated
2oz (50g) onion, peeled and grated
2 Grade 3 eggs, beaten
4 tblsp milk

1. Well butter a 2 pint (1¼ litre) casserole dish. Drain tomatoes, and reserve juice.
2. Crush tomatoes coarsely, mix with marjoram and spread over base of dish.
3. Sift flour, salt and mustard into a bowl. Rub in butter or margarine finely.
4. Toss in cheese and onion then mix to a stiffish consistency with the eggs and milk, stirring briskly with a fork. Avoid beating.
5. Spread smoothly over tomatoes in dish then bake 1 to 1¼ hours in oven centre set to 180°C (350°F), Gas 4. The pudding is cooked when a metal skewer, pushed gently into centre, comes out clean and dry. If not, return to oven for 10 more minutes or so.
6. Turn out on to a warm plate then serve with the tomato juice, heated until hot and seasoned to taste with salt, pepper and a dash of sugar.

Noodles in Creamy Blue Cheese Sauce

Serves 4 to 6

Using green noodles and a top quality blue cheese such as Stilton or Lymeswold, you have a memorable dish which is best accompanied with grilled or baked tomato halves.

8oz (225g) green noodles (flat and resembling ribbon)
1pt (575ml) boiling water
1 level tsp salt
1½oz (40g) butter or margarine
1½oz (40g) flour
½pt (275ml) milk
¼pt (150ml) single cream
1 Grade 3 egg, beaten
4oz (125g) Stilton or Lymeswold cheese, broken into small pieces
salt and pepper to taste

Topping
2oz (50g) Cheddar cheese, grated

1. Cook noodles in boiling water and salt for 8 to 10 minutes or until just tender. Drain and transfer to a well-buttered 3 pint (1¾ litre) heatproof dish.
2. To make sauce, melt butter or margarine in saucepan. Stir in flour to form a roux. Cook 1 minute without browning.
3. Gradually blend in milk and cream. Bring to boil, stirring. Simmer 2 minutes then gradually whisk in egg. Add cheese and stir over low heat until melted. Season.
4. Pour over noodles and toss gently with 2 spoons to mix. Sprinkle with Cheddar cheese and reheat and brown 15 minutes near top of oven set to 220°C (425°F), Gas 7. Spoon on to hot plates and serve straight away.

Eggs Chasseur

Serves 4 generously

Hunter's Eggs, to give the Chasseur bit an accurate translation, is a novel dish with a red wine sauce. It makes an ideal lunch or supper meal with a side salad of lettuce tossed in any dressing you choose.

1oz (25g) butter or margarine
2 tsp salad oil
3oz (75g) onion, peeled and finely chopped
6 medium trimmed mushrooms, washed and fairly finely chopped
1½ rounded tblsp flour
½pt (275ml) dry red wine
2 rounded tblsp tubed or canned tomato purée
1 level tsp light brown soft sugar
1 level tsp French mustard
2 tblsp brandy
1 to 1½ level tsp salt
1 level tblsp finely-chopped parsley
8 Grade 3 or 4 eggs, freshly poached
4 large slices freshly-made buttered toast

1. Heat butter or margarine and oil in saucepan. Add onions and mushrooms. Fry *gently* for 15 to 20 minutes or until onions are soft and just beginning to turn gold.
2. Stir in flour and cook 1½ minutes. Gradually blend in wine. Cook, stirring, until sauce comes to the boil and thickens. Mix in purée, sugar, mustard, brandy, salt and parsley. Simmer 3 minutes, stirring continually.
3. Place toast on 4 serving plates then stand 2 drained eggs on top of each. Coat each generously with the Chasseur sauce and serve straight away.

Steaks Chasseur

Serves 4

Make the Chasseur sauce as directed above. After it has simmered for 3 minutes, pour over freshly grilled steaks (rare, medium or well done, according to taste), and garnish each with a sprig of watercress.

High Rise Cheese Soufflé

Serves 4

A wondrous, high-in-the-sky soufflé fit for the very best of cooks. Follow directions carefully and you'll have a winner on your hands which partners happily with freshly-cooked baby carrots and mange tout tossed in butter.

2oz (50g) butter or margarine
2oz (50g) flour
½pt (275ml) milk
6oz (175g) mature Cheddar cheese, very finely grated
4 Grade 3 eggs, separated
½ level tsp salt
1 level tsp prepared English mustard
1 tsp lemon juice

1. Well-butter a 2½pt (1¼ litre) glass or pottery soufflé dish, about 7 ins (17½cm) in diameter. To support the soufflé as it rises, tie a strip of Bakewell non-stick parchment paper round the outside of the dish, making sure it stands 4 in (10cm) above top edge of dish. Set oven to 190°C (375°F), Gas 5.
2. Melt butter or margarine in a large saucepan. Mix in flour to form a roux. Cook 1 minute without browning, stirring all the time.
3. Gradually blend in milk. Cook, stirring, until mixture comes to the boil and thickens to a paste-like consistency, forming a

High-in-the-sky soufflé

ball in the centre of the pan and leaving sides clean.
4. Take off heat then beat in cheese and egg yolks. Season with salt and mustard and leave on one side temporarily.
5. Whisk egg whites and lemon juice to a stiff snow. Beat one-third into the cheese mixture to loosen it down a little then fold in rest of whites, gently and slowly, with a large metal spoon or spatula.
6. Pour mixture into prepared soufflé dish then bake for 45 minutes in oven centre. Under no account open the oven door or the soufflé will collapse.
7. Remove from oven, take to the table and gently remove Bakewell paper and eat at once as the soufflé falls quickly. To serve, spoon out on to warm plates.

High Rise Cheese and Chive Soufflé

Serves 4

Make as above but add 2 rounded tablespoons scissor-snipped chives at the same time as the cheese.

Dauphinoise Potatoes

Serves 4 to 6

Based on a classic dish from Geneva in Switzerland where the French influence prevails, this makes a nourishing and sustaining main course eaten with salad or cooked green vegetables to taste.

2lb (900g) potatoes, peeled and washed
12oz (350g) mixture of Gruyère and Emmenthal cheese, finely grated
¾pt (425ml) milk
3 Grade 3 eggs

large pinch of grated nutmeg
1 level tsp salt

Topping
2 rounded tblsp toasted breadcrumbs
1oz (25g) butter, melted

1. Well-butter a 3 pint (1¾ litre) casserole dish which is wide rather than deep; it should be about 10 ins (25cm) in diameter by about 4 ins (10cm) tall. Set oven to 190°C (325°F), Gas 5.
2. Halve potatoes and cook for 10 minutes only in boiling, salted water. Drain, rinse and wipe dry. Cut into ¼ in (just over ½cm) thick slices.
3. Fill dish with alternate layers of potatoes and cheese, reserving 2oz (50g) for topping. Begin and end with potatoes.
4. Beat milk, eggs, nutmeg and salt well together then pour into dish over potatoes and cheese.
5. Mix rest of cheese with breadcrumbs then sprinkle over top. Trickle with butter then bake, uncovered, 40 to 45 minutes just above oven centre.

Traditional Gratin Dauphinoise

Serves 6 to 8

Peel and wash 3lb (1½kg) old potatoes then grate into hair-thin slices. Alternatively do so with slicing attachment fitted to a food processor. Wash again and wring dry in tea towel. Fill a 12 ins (30cm) round buttered dish, of about 1 in (2½cm) in depth, with alternate layers of potatoes, 6oz (175g) grated Gruyère cheese and 3oz (75g) melted butter mixed with 1 peeled and crushed garlic clove and pepper to taste. Heat ½ pint (275ml) single cream until it just comes to the boil then pour down the side of dish in order not to disturb the layers. Sprinkle with 2oz (50g) more grated Gruyère cheese and bake, uncovered, for about 1 hour in oven centre set to 180°C (350°F), Gas 4. Serve with salad.

Pan Chicory with Eggs

Serves ·

Sometimes a vegetable meal with the addition of eggs makes a welcome contribution to the family diet, and this dish should prove popular as a sound all-rounder.

4 heads of chicory
2oz (50g) butter or margarine
2 large celery stalks, well-scrubbed and thinly sliced
4oz (125g) onion, peeled and coarsely grated
1lb (450g) washed potatoes, peeled and cut into dice
2 level tsp salt
1 tblsp lemon juice
3 tblsp dry white wine
4 Grade 3 eggs, freshly fried
2 heaped tblsp chopped parsley

1. Wash and dry chicory then remove and discard any outside leaves which are bruised and/or damaged. Remove a cone shaped core from the base of each head and discard. This is usually the bitter part of the vegetable and not worth eating.
2. Cut into slices with a stainless knife. Heat butter or margarine in a pan. Add chicory, celery and onion.
3. Fry over a moderate heat until pale gold. Mix in potatoes, salt, lemon juice and wine. Cover. Cook over a low heat, stirring occasionally, for 30 minutes.
4. Spoon out on to 4 warm plates, top each with a fried egg and sprinkle with parsley.

Fennel in Mornay Sauce

Serves ·

Florence fennel, pale green and white, is a vegetable with the subtle tang of aniseed. It is admirable in cheese sauce and makes a nutritious meal for those on the vegetarian bandwagon.

1½lb (675g) Florence fennel
cold water
2 tblsp lemon juice
1½ level tsp salt
1½oz (40g) butter or margarine
1½oz (40g) flour
½pt (275ml) single cream
6oz (175g) red Leicester cheese, grated
1 level tsp mild English mustard
salt and pepper to taste
1oz (25g) extra butter, melted
2 level tblsp breadcrumbs

1. Trim fennel, removing the 'fronds'. Wash then put into a large pan. Add cold water, lemon juice and salt.
2. Bring to boil, lower heat and cover. Simmer for about 45 minutes or until tender. Drain, reserving ½pt (275ml) water.
3. Melt butter or margarine in a pan. Add flour and cook 2 minutes. Gradually blend in fennel water, followed by cream.
4. Cook, stirring, until sauce comes to boil and thickens. Remove from heat. Mix in 4oz (125g) cheese, mustard and salt and pepper to taste.
5. Slice fennel and put into a fairly shallow, greased heatproof dish. Coat with sauce then sprinkle rest of cheese on top. Spoon butter over cheese then dot with crumbs. Brown under a hot grill.

Duck with Carefree Orange Sauce

Serves 4

Taking the easy way out of a top class meal is something we have to do occasionally, and the recipe below shows you how it can be done.

93

1 by 4lb (2kg) oven ready duck, thawed if frozen and giblet bag
   removed
1 can ready-to-serve oxtail soup
juice of 1 medium orange
juice of 1 medium lemon
1 level tblsp redcurrant jelly
washed and dried peel of ½ medium orange, cut into hair-thin
   strips
2 tblsp brandy or whisky
salt and pepper to taste
1 peeled and sliced orange for garnishing

1. To make serving easier later, cut duck into 4 joints and prick
   skin all over with a fork to allow fat to run freely.
2. Place on rack in roasting tin, skin sides uppermost, to form a
   single layer. Roast 1 hour or until tender, standing tin 1 shelf
   above oven centre. The temperature should be 200°C
   (400°F), Gas 6.
3. Place crisp and well-browned duck in a dish to keep hot. To
   make sauce, put soup into a pan with all remaining
   ingredients except alcohol and seasoning.
4. Whisk over a low heat until sauce comes to a gentle boil and
   begins to bubble. Continue to cook until redcurrant jelly
   completely dissolves.
5. Warm alcohol in a separate pan and flame. Mix into sauce
   then season to taste with salt and pepper. Pour over duck
   and decorate with orange slices.

Turkey Rolls

Serves 4

With turkey breast fillets readily available from most supermarket chains and some butcher shops, finding them is no
problem and this dish is one way of making them both appetising
and appealing.

4 turkey breast fillets, each 3 to 4oz (75 to 125g)
4oz (125g) lean minced raw beef or unsmoked gammon, finely
  minced
4oz (125g) onions, finely grated
1oz (25g) fresh white breadcrumbs
1 rounded tsp parsley
½ level tsp mixed herbs
1 Grade 3 egg, beaten
1½oz (40g) butter or margarine
¼pt (150ml) chicken stock
¼pt (150ml) dry red wine
1 level tsp salt
pepper to taste
1 level tblsp cornflour
2 tblsp cold water

1. Beat turkey fillets between 2 sheets of greaseproof paper until very thin. The best implement to use is a rolling pin.
2. Mix together minced beef or gammon, the onions, crumbs, parsley and herbs. Bind with the beaten egg.
3. Put equal amounts on to the turkey fillets then fold edges over filling to form parcels. Tie in 2 or 3 places with fine string to hold rolls together.
4. Heat butter in a saucepan. Add turkey rolls and fry briskly until well-browned all over, turning with 2 spoons.
5. Pour stock and wine into saucepan. Add salt and pepper to taste. Bring to boil and lower heat. Simmer 30 to 35 minutes or until turkey is tender.
6. Lift out of pan and cut off string. Arrange in small serving dish and keep hot.
7. To thicken gravy, blend cornflour smoothly with water. Pour into pan and cook, stirring, until mixture comes to the boil and thickens.
8. Adjust seasoning to taste and pour over rolls. Serve hot with creamed potatoes and a selection of cooked vegetables to taste.

Curried Apple Turkey with Wine

Serves 4

Many is the time one has leftover turkey and the eternal sandwiches can be extremely boring. Here is an interesting way of pepping up cold cooked turkey in a light, almost perfumed curry sauce that is in its element served with rice and assorted side dishes (or sambals) of chutney, natural yogurt flavoured with salt and chopped mint, and sliced banana sprinkled with lemon juice.

1oz (25g) butter or margarine
2 tsp salad oil
6oz (175g) onion, peeled and very thinly sliced
3 level tsp mild curry powder
1oz (25g) flour
¼pt (150ml) single cream
4oz (125g) natural yogurt
1 garlic clove, peeled and crushed
2 level tblsp tubed or canned tomato purée
½ level tsp garam masala (curry seasoning powder)
1 level tsp salt
2 tblsp fresh lime juice
4 dessert apples, peeled and sliced
1 rounded tblsp fruit chutney
12oz to 1lb (350 to 450g) cold cooked turkey cut into large dice

1. Melt butter or margarine and salad oil in a saucepan. Add onion and fry gently until warm gold.
2. Mix in curry powder and flour and cook a further minute. Blend in cream and yogurt then bring to boil, stirring all the time.
3. Add garlic, purée, garam masala, salt, lime juice, apples and chutney. Bring to boil, cover then simmer over a low heat for 30 minutes.
4. Stir in turkey and cover. Continue to boil gently, stirring occasionally, for a further 20 minutes.

Cheesy Turkey Fillets Holstein   *Serves 4*

An impressive way of presenting turkey breast fillets and delicious with sauté potatoes and a green salad.

4 turkey breast fillets, each 4 to 6oz (125 to 175g), washed and dried

4 level tblsp flour } mixed
½ level tsp salt

1 Grade 1 or 2 egg, well-beaten

5 rounded tblsp lightly-toasted breadcrumbs } mixed
3 rounded tblsp grated Parmesan cheese

3oz (75g) butter or margarine

1 tblsp salad oil

4 freshly fried eggs

4 wedges of lemon

1. Beat turkey fillets until wafer thin with a rolling pin then snip round the edges with scissors to prevent them curling as they cook.
2. Dust with flour and salt then dip each fillet in the beaten egg. Toss in crumb and cheese mixture and leave to stand for 20 minutes for the coating to settle and set. Lift up each one and shake off surplus crumbs and cheese.
3. To cook, heat butter or margarine and oil in large frying pan. Fry turkey fillets, one at a time, for 8 to 10 minutes, turning once.
4. Lift out to drain on a plate lined with crumpled kitchen paper and keep hot. Repeat with remaining 3 fillets.
5. Transfer to 4 warm dinner plates and top each with a freshly fried egg. Garnish with lemon. Serve straight away.

Gammon Holstein

Serves 4

Make as above but use 4 gammon steaks, also snipped round the edges, instead of the turkey.

Crispy Gammon with Redcurrant Peaches

Serves 4

Make as first recipe above, using 4 gammon steaks instead of turkey fillets and snipping round the edges to prevent curling. Coat in 8 rounded tablespoons lightly-toasted breadcrumbs and no cheese. Fry and drain as directed then top each with a canned and drained peach half, filled with redcurrant jelly.

Sesame Chicken

Serves 4

Crackling with sesame seeds and flavoured with mustard, this is an unusual way of preparing chicken and is admirable served with a full-blown mixed salad topped, in Greek style, with squares of Feta cheese and a trickle of olive oil.

4 large chicken joints
1pt (575ml) water
2 level tsp salt
1 large onion, peeled
1 bouquet garni bag
mild French or German mustard
4 heaped tblsp sesame seeds
2oz (50g) butter or margarine

1. Wash chicken then put into a pan with water, salt, onion (left whole), and bouquet garni bag.
2. Bring to boil and skim. Lower heat and cover. Simmer until chicken is just tender, allowing about 30 minutes.
3. Remove from pan and leave to drain. Set oven to 200°C (400°F), Gas 6.
4. Spread skin sides of joints with mustard then transfer to

baking tray. Sprinkle closely with sesame seeds. Bake 30 minutes just above oven centre. Serve with fried potatoes and the salad described above.

Saffron Chicken with Wine   *Serves 8*

Stylish and somewhat Spanish in character, this chicken dish is useful to keep handy when planning to entertain dinner guests.

8 large chicken joints
flour
2oz (50g) butter or margarine
2 tblsp olive or corn oil
12oz (350g) onions
6 celery stalks, scrubbed and sliced
1 can (14oz or 400g) tomatoes
¼pt (150ml) chicken stock (use a cube and water)
½ level tsp saffron strands
2oz (50g) green stuffed olives, halved
seasoning to taste
1 tblsp brandy

1. Wash and dry chicken then coat all over with flour. Heat butter or margarine and oil in pan. Add chicken and fry briskly until well-browned on both sides, turning twice.
2. Remove to plate temporarily. Add onions and celery to remaining fat and oil in pan and fry until a deep gold. Turn often to prevent burning.
3. Add tomatoes to pan and crush against sides. Stir in stock, saffron, olives and seasoning to taste. Bring to boil and replace chicken.
4. Cover and simmer about 45 minutes or until chicken is tender. Warm brandy in small pan then ignite. Pour into pan over chicken.

5. Transfer to a warm serving dish and serve hot with boiled potatoes and a mixed salad.

Chicken in Paprika Cream Sauce *Serves 4*

Capturing the mood of the Astro-Hungarian Empire, this creamy orange-coloured chicken dish makes a gracious meal for family and friends and if you double all the ingredients, you will find there is adequate for eight servings.

4 large chicken joints
flour
3 tblsp salad oil
8oz (225g) onions, peeled and chopped
1 rounded tblsp paprika
5oz (150g) tubed or canned tomato purée
1 level tsp salt
1 level tsp caster sugar
½pt (275ml) boiling chicken stock
1 carton (5oz or 142ml) soured cream

1. Wash and dry chicken joints and dust lightly with flour. Heat oil in pan. Add chicken and fry briskly until golden brown, turning twice.
2. Remove to plate for time being. Add onions to pan and fry until pale gold. Mix in paprika, purée, salt, sugar and stock. Bring to boil, stirring.
3. Replace chicken and cover. Simmer about 45 minutes or until tender, stirring occasionally.
4. Lift chicken out of pan into a warm serving dish. Whisk soured cream into tomato sauce, reheat and pour over chicken.

101

Chicken and Peppers in Paprika Cream Sauce

Serves 4

Make as above, but first de-seed one washed and dried medium green pepper and cut flesh into strips. Fry with the onions.

Tandoori Chicken

Serves 4

Cooked in a Tandoor (a special clay oven) in its country of origin, a fair copy can be made in an ordinary oven with the right blend of flavourings and spices.

8 medium chicken joints, skinned
8oz (225g) natural yogurt
8oz (225g) onions, peeled and finely grated
2 garlic cloves, peeled and crushed
1 level tsp ginger
2 level tsp salt
4 level tsp medium hot curry powder
4 level tsp paprika
4 tsp malt vinegar
4 tsp Worcester sauce
1 tsp chili sauce (only for hot Tandoori)
2 rounded tblsp tubed or canned tomato purée
juice of 1 large lemon

To Serve
lettuce leaves
wedges of tomatoes
wedges of lemon
1 large onion, peeled and thinly sliced

1. Place chicken joints, flesh sides uppermost, in large and shallow dish. Make sure they form a single layer.

2. Beat all remaining ingredients well together for marinade and spoon over chicken. Cover dish securely with clingfilm and refrigerate 12 hours.
3. Before cooking, stand on rack in roasting tin and coat heavily with marinade.
4. Bake 1¼ to 1½ hours just above oven centre set to 180°C (350°F), Gas 4. Baste with marinade 2 or 3 times.
5. Line a shallow serving dish with lettuce. Top with Tandoori chicken then add tomatoes, lemon and onion slices separated into rings. Accompany with Indian bread (sometimes available from Oriental shops) or Pitta bread.

Bolognese Chicken

Serves about 6

Chicken in a kind of meatless Bolognese sauce combines two old faithfuls and turns them into an appetising chicken dish which teams best with rice or pasta.

6 large chicken joints or 1 × 3lb (1½kg) chicken, cut into 6
    pieces
flour
2oz (50g) butter or margarine
2 tsp salad oil
3oz (75g) gammon, chopped
8oz (225g) onions, peeled and chopped
2 garlic cloves, peeled and finely chopped or crushed
1 can (14oz or 200g) tomatoes
1 heaped tblsp tubed or canned tomato purée
1 level tblsp dark brown soft sugar
1 level tsp salt
1 level tsp marjoram
1 level tsp basil
2 rounded tblsp finely-chopped parsley

103

1. Skin chicken then wash and dry joints. Coat all over with flour then lift up each piece and shake off surplus.
2. Heat butter and oil in large saucepan. Add chicken joints and fry briskly until brown on both sides. Remove to plate for time being.
3. Add gammon, onions and garlic to pan. Fry until warm gold. Stir in the tomatoes, purée, sugar, salt, marjoram, basil and half the parsley.
4. Replace chicken and make sure all pieces are well-coated with tomato mixture. Bring to boil, stirring gently.
5. Lower heat and cover pan. Simmer gently for about 1 hour or until chicken is tender.
6. Spoon into a serving dish and sprinkle rest of parsley on top. Serve with freshly-cooked rice or pasta.

Devilled Drumsticks

Serves 4

Sold in packs by supermarket chains and freezer centres, chicken drumsticks make an appetising meal, especially when devilled and served with baked jacket potatoes and sweetcorn.

12 chicken drumsticks, thawed if frozen
1 level tblsp powder mustard
2 level tsp curry powder
2 level tsp paprika
¼ level tsp cayenne pepper (omit for less fiery taste)
½ level tsp salt
2oz (50g) butter or margarine, melted

1. Wash and dry drumsticks.
2. Mix together mustard and curry powders, paprika and cayenne pepper then the salt.
3. Coat drumsticks with the spicy powder and put into a greased baking tin.

4. Baste with the melted butter or margarine then bake, uncovered, for 30 to 35 minutes just above oven centre set to 200°C (400°F) Gas 6, turning once.

Chicken Marengo   *Serves 4*

There are now so many versions of this typically Italian chicken dish that it is hard to know which is the genuine article and, like many Italian foods, I am sure the recipe varies from family to family. This is one variation served with fried bread.

4 medium chicken joints, each divided into 2 pieces
flour for coating
4 tblsp salad oil
2 garlic cloves, peeled and crushed
1lb (450g) blanched tomatoes, skinned and chopped
2 level tblsp tubed or canned tomato purée
½pt (275ml) dry white wine
3 level tblsp chopped parsley
salt and pepper to taste

To Serve
4 large slices white bread
2oz (50g) butter or margarine for frying

1. Wash and dry chicken pieces then coat with flour. Heat oil in a large frying pan or fairly wide saucepan.
2. Add chicken and fry until crisp and golden, turning twice. Remove to plate temporarily.
3. Add garlic, tomatoes, purée, wine and half the parsley to remaining oil in pan. Season to taste with salt and pepper and stir well to mix.
4. Bring to boil and replace chicken with any leftover flour. Cover. Simmer about 45 minutes or until tender.
5. Transfer to a warm dish and sprinkle with rest of parsley. To finish, cut bread into triangles or halves and fry in the butter or margarine until golden brown.
6. Arrange round the chicken and serve straight away. Accompany with pasta.

Coq au Vin

Serves 4

Always in fashion, Coq au Vin is the chic one from France, which, like Boeuf Bourguignonne, is cooked in red wine and best accompanied by boiled potatoes and green vegetables such as peas or mange tout, braised celery and French beans. Or you can choose a salad.

1 × 3lb (1½kg) chicken, cut into 4 joints
1oz (25g) flour
2oz (50g) butter or margarine
3 tsp salad oil
4oz (125g) gammon, chopped
8oz (225g) onions, peeled and chopped
1 medium carrot, peeled and thinly sliced
1 garlic clove, peeled and chopped
12 shallots or small onions, peeled and left whole
1 bouquet garni bag
1 level tsp salt
½pt (275ml) dry red wine
8oz (225g) washed and dried mushrooms, thinly sliced
1 tblsp brandy
2 rounded tblsp parsley

1. Wash and dry chicken then coat all over with flour.
2. Heat butter or margarine and oil in a pan. Add chicken and fry briskly on both sides until golden. Remove to plate temporarily.
3. Add gammon, onions, carrot and garlic to pan and fry over a medium heat until pale gold, stirring from time to time and allowing about 10 minutes.
4. Add shallots or small onions, the bouquet garni bag, salt and wine. Bring to boil, stirring. Replace chicken.
5. Lower heat and cover. Simmer about 50 minutes or until tender. Add mushrooms and continue to cook a further 15 minutes. Remove bouquet garni bag.
6. Warm brandy in a small pan and ignite. Stir into chicken and gravy. Transfer to a warm serving dish and sprinkle with parsley.

Rabbit Stew with Lemon Dumplings

Serves 4 to 6

Anyone who enjoys rabbit will appreciate this dish, simmered as it is in red wine and served with fluffy lemon dumplings.

1 medium-sized rabbit
3 level tblsp flour
2oz (50g) lard or margarine
4oz (125g) *each*, onion, carrot and turnip, peeled
1 medium celery stalk, well-scrubbed
½pt (275ml) dry red wine
¼pt (150ml) water
2 level tsp caster sugar
1 level tsp salt
1 bouquet garni bag

Dumplings
4oz (125g) self-raising flour

1½oz (40g) margarine
½ level tsp salt
1 level tsp finely-grated lemon peel
about 4 tblsp cold milk to mix

1. Cut rabbit into joints and soak in cold salted water to which a little juice has been added. This not only whitens the flesh but reduces any likelihood of a strong taste. Leave 2 hours then drain. Wipe dry and coat with flour.

2. Heat lard or margarine in a large pan. Add rabbit and fry all over until golden brown and crisp. Remove to a plate for the time being.

3. Dice onion, carrot and turnip and add to pan. Fry gently until pale gold, turning from time to time. Allow about 15 to 20 minutes with lid on pan.

4. Add wine, water, sugar, salt and bouquet garni bag then bring to boil, stirring. Replace rabbit and any remaining flour.

5. Cover and simmer gently for about 2 hours or until rabbit is tender. Remove bouquet garni bag.

6. About 30 minutes before ready, sift flour into a bowl for dumplings. Rub in margarine then toss in salt and lemon peel. Mix to a soft dough with the milk, using a fork for mixing.

7. Roll into 8 balls and put on top of stew. Cover and continue cooking until ready; the dunplings will take about 20 minutes to puff up. Accompany with creamed potatoes and green vegetables to taste.

Rabbit Stew Espagnole *Serves 4 to 6*

Make exactly as previous recipe but fry 2oz (50g) chopped lean bacon with the vegetables, add 2 rounded tablespoons tubed or canned tomato purée with the wine and, instead of dumplings, add 4oz (125g) trimmed and washed button mushrooms to the stew about 10 minutes before the end of cooking time.

Bobotie

Serves

A colourful and delicious South African lamb dish.

3oz (75g) seedless raisins
3oz (75g) flaked almonds
3 large slices white bread, decrusted
4 tblsp boiling water
1oz (25g) margarine
4oz (125g) onion, peeled and chopped
2lb (900g) raw lamb, cut from leg then diced and minced
2 level tsp salt
3 level tsp light brown soft sugar
2 level tblsp mild curry powder
4 tblsp lemon juice
6oz (175g) fruit chutney
3 Grade 3 eggs
½pt (275ml) milk

1. Soak seedless raisins in enough boiling water to cover while preparing other ingredients. Toast almonds in oven set to 200°C (400°F), Gas 6 for 10 to 15 minutes or until light brown. Cool.
2. Cube bread and put into basin. Cover with water. Leave on one side for the time being.
3. Heat margarine in saucepan. Mix in onion and fry until a warm gold. Tip into mixing bowl. Add lamb, drained raisins, soaked bread, 1½ level teaspoon salt, sugar, curry powder, lemon juice and chutney.
4. Mix thoroughly then transfer to 3 pint (1¾ litre) greased ovenproof dish, spreading it smoothly with a knife. Sprinkle with half the almonds.

110

5. Beat eggs and milk well together and season with last ½ teaspoon of salt. Pour over lamb in dish then coat with remaining almonds.
6. Cover with lightly-greased foil and bake 45 minutes in oven centre. Uncover and continue to bake a further 30 to 40 minutes or until well-browned and cooked through. Serve with freshly cooked rice and extra chutney.

Lamb Curry with Spice Rice   *Serves 6*

A fine-flavoured and authentic-tasting curry with an accompaniment of exotically spiced long grain rice.

4 tblsp corn oil
1½lb (675g) leg of lamb (boned weight), diced and with all fat removed
8oz (225g) onions, peeled and quartered
1 garlic clove, peeled and crushed
2 level tsp *each*, ground ginger and paprika
1 level tsp *each*, ground coriander and cumin
½ level tsp chili powder (use more if you like a fiery curry)
4 cardamon pods
3 cloves
5 peppercorns
¾pt (425ml) beef stock (use cubes and water)
5oz (150ml) natural yogurt

Rice
8oz (225g) American long grain rice
1pt (575ml) beef stock (use cubes and water), boiling
1 level tsp turmeric
½ level tsp cinnamon
5 cloves
4 cardamons
salt and pepper to taste

1. Heat oil in large pan. Add lamb and fry cubes briskly until golden brown all over. Remove to plate temporarily.
2. Add onions and garlic to remaining oil in pan and fry until pale gold, turning frequently to prevent sticking. Add ginger, paprika, coriander, cumin, chili powder, cardamon, cloves, peppercorns and stock. Bring to boil. Replace lamb.
3. Lower heat and cover pan. Simmer 1½ to 2 hours or until lamb is tender and curry sauce has thickened as the mixture has cooked down. Stir occasionally to prevent sticking. Mix in yogurt.
4. About 25 minutes before curry is ready, put rice and all remaining ingredients into a pan. Stand over medium heat and stir round twice or three times as it boils.
5. Lower heat and cover. Cook 20 minutes or until rice grains are plump and tender and have absorbed all the liquid. Put into a dish and serve with the curry. Accompany with bowls of chopped hard-boiled egg, mango chutney, diced cucumber mixed with yogurt, and any hot pickle such as lime or chili.

Curried Lamb Korma   *Serves 6*

A mild, delicate but finely flavoured curry for those who like Oriental cooking to be gentle and not fiery.

2oz (50g) butter or Indian ghee (pronounced gee as in Gertie!)
8oz (225g) onions, peeled and chopped
2 garlic cloves, peeled and crushed
3lb (1½kg) leg of lamb, meat cut off bone and cubed
1oz (25g) flour
1 to 2 level tblsp of the mildest curry you can find
8oz (225g) blanched tomatoes, skinned and chopped
1 rounded tblsp tubed or canned tomato purée made up to ¼pt
   (150ml) with hot water
1 carton (5oz or 150g) natural yogurt

3 rounded tblsp soured or double cream
1 tblsp fresh lemon juice (use half with soured cream)
2 to 3 level tsp salt
3 level tblsp desiccated coconut

1. Heat butter or ghee in fairly large pan. Add onion and garlic and fry over medium heat until golden.
2. Dust lamb all over with flour and add to pan. Fry until lightly browned.
3. Stir in all remaining ingredients. Bring to boil, lower heat and cover. Simmer gently 1½ hours, stirring occasionally to prevent sticking.
4. Cool down completely and refrigerate overnight. Before serving, remove any solid fat that has risen to the top. Bring to boil and bubble gently for 15 minutes.
5. Serve with freshly boiled rice and side dishes of cubed cucumber, sliced onions and tomatoes, mango chutney and lime pickle.

Kashmir Style Fruited Curry   *Serves 6*

A little hotter than the Korma, this is a fragrant curry packed with fruit and nuts.

Make exactly as recipe above but omit coconut. Instead, add 4 oz (125g) well-washed and sliced apricots, 1oz (25g) raisins and 2oz (50g) blanched and halved almonds. Serve with the same accompaniments.

Middle Eastern Kofta Kebabs   *Serves 4*

These are kebabs of minced lamb, typical of Middle East

cooking and appetisingly spiced. Serve them with freshly boiled rice and a salad of peppers, tomatoes and onions, all coarsely chopped and tossed with French dressing.

1lb (450g) leg of lamb (boned weight), diced
4oz (125g) onion, peeled and cut into eighths
1 Grade 3 egg
½ level tsp ground cumin
1 level tsp salt
1 level tsp oregano
½ level tsp cayenne pepper (fiery and therefore optional)
2 level tblsp flour

1. Mince lamb and onion finely together (or do this in a food processor) then put into a mixing bowl.
2. Stir in all remaining ingredients. Mould into sausage roll shapes round 8 short metal skewers.
3. Place in lightly greased grill pan and grill about 10 minutes, turning 3 times. Serve on a bed of rice.

Moussaka

Serves 6

One of the Grecian dishes everyone remembers. Delicious by itself or with a large mixed salad topped, in classic style, with pieces of Feta cheese and a trickle of olive oil.

2 large aubergines, left unpeeled but washed and dried
3 tblsp salad oil
6oz (175g) onions, peeled and finely chopped
1 garlic clove, peeled and very thinly sliced
12oz (350g) uncooked lamb, cut from the fillet end of the leg and finely minced
3 tblsp dry white wine
4oz (125g) blanched tomatoes, skinned and chopped
1 rounded tblsp tubed or canned tomato purée

½ level tsp oregano
4 tblsp water
salt and pepper to taste

For topping
1oz (25g) butter or margarine
1oz (25g) flour
½pt (275ml) milk
4oz (125g) Cheddar cheese, finely grated
⅛ tsp nutmeg
1 egg yolk
white pepper to taste

1. Cut green tops of aubergines and discard. Slice vegetables thinly and place on a large board or plate in a single layer. Sprinkle thickly with salt and leave to stand 30 minutes or until large drops of moisture appear on the surface. Turn over and repeat. (This stops aubergine absorbing too much oil.) Rinse, drain and wipe dry.
2. Heat oil in a large frying pan. Add aubergine slices, a few at a time, and fry fairly briskly until light golden on both sides. Remove to a plate covered with crumpled kitchen paper which will soak up excess oil.
3. Add onions and garlic to pan, adding a little extra oil if there is none left in the pan (aubergines tend to be greedy!). Fry until golden brown. Mix in lamb and continue to stir-fry until well-browned and crumbly.
4. Add wine, tomatoes, purée, oregano, water and salt and pepper to taste to meat mixture. Simmer 3 minutes then leave aside temporarily.
5. To make sauce, melt butter or margarine in a pan. Stir in flour to form a roux. Gradually blend in milk.
6. Cook, stirring, until sauce comes to the boil and thickens. Gently whisk in remaining ingredients.
7. To assemble, fill a medium-sized and greased ovenproof dish with alternate layers of fried aubergine slices and lamb

mixture.

8. Coat with sauce then reheat and brown 30 to 40 minutes just above oven centre set to 220°C (425°F), Gas 7. Spoon out on to plates to serve.

Pork and Onion Kebabs   *Serves 4 generously*

Chinese-style pork on skewers — it's different anyway and fun for entertaining!

2lb (900g) pork fillet
4 small onions (8oz or 225g), peeled

Marinade
4 tblsp soy sauce
2 tblsp clear honey
1 tblsp salad oil
1 slightly rounded tblsp finely-chopped spring onion
2 level tsp ground ginger

To serve
½ head of iceberg lettuce
1 medium onion, peeled and sliced then each slice separated into rings

1. Trim fat off pork and cut meat into 1 in (2½cm) cubes. Cut each onion into quarters.
2. Beat all marinade ingredients well together in bowl. Arrange meat and onion quarters, in single layer, in shallow dish.
3. Coat with marinade. Cover with cling film and leave to stand at kitchen temperature for 3 hours.
4. Thread pork and onion quarters on to 4 long skewers and grill 20 minutes, turning several times and basting with leftover marinade.
5. Arrange on a bed of lettuce with onion rings. Accompany with freshly cooked American long grain rice.

Baked Pork Chop 'Sandwich'   *Serves 4*

Provided you have no objection to attending to vegetables,

these pork chops will reward you well in flavour and tenderness. The only accompaniment necessary is a mixed salad or cooked green vegetables to taste.

2oz (50g) margarine
4 pork chops, each 6 to 8oz (175 to 225g), trimmed of excess fat
8oz (225g) onion, peeled and finely chopped
1lb (450g) washed potatoes, peeled and grated (raw)
1 can condensed cream of celery soup
3 tblsp milk
pepper to taste
1oz (25g) butter or margarine, melted

1. Heat margarine in pan. Add chops and fry on both sides until well-browned. Remove to a plate for time being.
2. Add onion to rest of margarine in pan and fry gently until golden.
3. Set oven to 200°C (400°F), Gas 6. Cover base of fairly shallow, oblong greased ovenproof dish with half the potatoes.
4. Top with chops and all the fried onions. Cover with rest of potatoes.
5. Heat soup in pan with milk and pepper to taste. Pour evenly into dish over top layer of potatoes. Trickle with melted butter or margarine then bake, uncovered, for 45 minutes just above oven centre.

Easy-Style Vitello Tonnato   *Serves 6 to 8*

If made authentically, the veal used for this Italian speciality should be simmered with anchovies, canned tuna, vegetables, wine and seasonings and then served sliced, ice cold, in a sauce made from the cooking liquor plus egg yolks and capers. For those of us who find time a precious commodity, I present my short-cut version and in view of the difficulty in finding roasting veal, you can substitute cold roast pork or turkey breast instead.

¾pt (425ml) mayonnaise
1 can (about 7oz or 200g) tuna, mashed finely in its own oil
2oz (50g) onion, peeled and coarsely chopped
6 anchovy fillets in oil, drained
cold chicken stock (use cubes and water)
1 rounded tblsp capers, well-drained
salt and pepper to taste
1½lb (675g) *cooked* weight of cold roast veal, pork or turkey breast
1 large lemon, cut into thin wedges

1. Spoon mayonnaise into blender or food processor. Add tuna, onion and anchovy fillets. Run machine until mixture is smooth.
2. Transfer to a mixing bowl and thin down to a thickish pouring consistency (like very rich, unbeaten double cream) with the stock, beating it in bit by bit.
3. Mix in the capers then season to taste with salt and pepper.
4. To complete, slice meat or turkey thinly then arrange in layers, with the tuna sauce between, in a shallow serving dish.
5. End with a layer of sauce, covering meat or turkey completely. Refrigerate overnight, garnish with lemon and serve with a mixed salad.

Pacific Ocean Pork

Serves 4

A sweet-sour pork dish which comes from the area of the Philippines.

1lb (450g) stewing pork, diced (weight without fat or bone)
4oz (125g) green pepper, washed and dried
4oz (125g) onion, peeled
2 tblsp corn or ground nut oil
1 garlic clove, peeled and crushed
1oz (25g) dark brown soft sugar
¼ level tsp cayenne pepper (hot, so omit if preferred)
½pt (275ml) chicken stock (use cubes and water)
2 tblsp vinegar
2 tblsp soy sauce
1 level tblsp cornflour
1 tblsp cold water
½ level tsp salt

1. Wash and dry pork and leave on one side for the moment. Split pepper, remove inside fibres and seeds and cut flesh into strips. Chop onion very finely.
2. Heat oil in a pan until hot. Add pork dice and fry briskly until well-browned and sealed. Remove to plate. Add pepper strips, chopped onion and garlic to remaining oil in pan. Fry over medium heat until golden.
3. Replace pork then stir in sugar, cayenne pepper if used, stock, vinegar and soy sauce. Bring to boil, stirring. Lower heat and cover pan.
4. Simmer gently for about 1 to 1¼ hours or until pork is tender. To thicken, mix cornflour smoothly with water. Add

to pan and stir until gravy bubbles up to the boil. Stir in salt.
5. Simmer 5 minutes then serve with rice or noodles.

Stuffed Peppers Parmagiani

Serves 6

A warm-hearted and vibrant stuffed pepper dish which can be served hot or lightly chilled.

6 large red peppers
boiling water
2 tblsp salad oil
6oz (175g) onions, peeled and chopped
8oz (225g) lean minced raw beef
6oz (175g) American long grain rice
¾pt (425ml) hot stock (use beef cubes and water)
salt and pepper to taste
2 slightly rounded tblsp grated Parmesan cheese

Sauce
¾pt (425ml) tomato juice
5oz (150g) tubed or canned tomato purée
1 medium onion, peeled and grated
1 garlic clove, peeled and crushed
2 level tsp dark brown soft sugar
1 level tsp salt
1 level tsp oregano
1 tblsp brandy

1. Cut tops off peppers and remove inside fibres and seeds. Place peppers in deepish pan with tops and cover with boiling water. Leave to stand 5 minutes to soften. Drain well and pat dry with paper towels.
2. For filling, heat oil in pan. Add onions and fry until light gold. Mix in minced beef and stir over medium heat until meat browns. Add rice, stock and salt and pepper to taste.
3. Bring to boil and lower heat. Stir round with fork then cover. Simmer 15 minutes or until rice is tender and has absorbed the liquid. Mix in cheese.
4. Spoon into peppers then stand upright and close together in a deepish ovenproof dish. Add tops.
5. For sauce, put all ingredients into a pan and bring just up to the boil. Pour into dish, basting the peppers with sauce as you do so.
6. Bake 30 minutes, uncovered, just above oven centre set to 375°F (190°C), Gas 5. Baste several times. Serve hot or cold with sauce.

Beef and Lady Finger Casserole   *Serves 8*

Temptingly Middle-Eastern in character, this dish is based on minced beef and okra (now more generally available from vegetable markets, supermarket chains and oriental grocers), casseroled in the oven. Serve it with rice or boiled potatoes and accompany with a mixed salad tossed with yogurt dressing.

1½lb (675g) fresh okra (ladies fingers)
3oz (75g) butter or margarine
2 tsp olive oil
2lb (900g) lean minced beef
6oz (175g) onion, peeled and finely grated
2 garlic cloves, peeled and crushed
5oz (150g) tubed or canned tomato purée
1 level tsp salt

pepper to taste
¾pt (425ml) beef stock (use cubes and water)
lemon slices for garnishing

1. Top and tail okra then wash well and dry thoroughly. Heat half the butter or margarine in a large frying pan. Add okra and fry gently for about 20 minutes, carefully turning with 2 spoons.
2. Remove from pan and put on to a plate lined with kitchen paper. Leave on one side for time being.
3. Add remaining butter or margarine and oil to pan. Mix in beef, onion and garlic. Cook over a low heat, fork-stirring all the time, until beef is crumbly and light brown; 8 to 10 minutes.
4. Add salt, pepper and half the stock. Cook over a fairly high heat, stirring continuously, until most of the liquid has been driven off.
5. Fill a well-greased 3 pint (1¾ litre) ovenproof casserole with alternate layers of okra and minced beef mixture. Pour in rest of stock then cover dish with lid or foil.
6. Bake 1 hour just above oven centre set to 190°C (375°F), Gas 5. Spoon out of dish on to warm plates.

Speedy Spag Bol

Serves 4

For all lovers of Spaghetti Bolognese, this one is blessed with an extra speedy sauce using store cupboard ingredients plus fresh beef.

12oz (350g) raw minced beef
1 can (14oz or 400g) tomatoes
¼ level tsp garlic granules
1 level tsp salt
2 level tblsp red and green dried pepper flakes
2 level tblsp dried onion flakes or slices
1 level tsp basil or mixed herbs
¼pt (150ml) water

1. Put beef into a pan and fry over a medium heat, stirring all the time, until brown and crumbly.
2. Mix in remaining ingredients and bring to boil, stirring. Lower heat and cover.
3. Simmer 1 hour to amalgamate flavours then spoon over freshly cooked spaghetti, allowing about 3oz (75g) raw weight per person. Pass grated Parmesan cheese separately.

Green Noodle Bolognese

Serves 4

For a change of scene, serve the sauce above with freshly-cooked green ribbon noodles (Tagliatelle).

Beef Crumble

Serves 4

A simple beef stew converted into something much more interesting by being given a crumble topping.

1½lb (675g) braising steak, washed and dried
1½oz (40g) flour
1½oz (40g) butter or margarine
4oz (125g) *each* onion, carrot and turnip or parsnip, peeled and thinly sliced
¾pt (425ml) water
1½ level tsp salt
pepper to taste

Crumble
6oz (175g) plain flour
1 level tsp powder mustard
1 level tsp salt

3oz (75g) butter or margarine
½ level tsp thyme

1. Cube beef then coat with flour. Heat butter or margarine in a saucepan. Add beef and fry briskly until well browned and sealed. Remove to a plate for the time being.
2. Add vegetables to remaining fat in pan and fry, covered, for 15 to 20 minutes. Replace meat, with any leftover flour, then pour in water.
3. Season to taste with salt and pepper then bring to boil, stirring. Lower heat and cover. Simmer about 1½ hours or until meat is tender. Remove from heat and cool completely.
4. Put meat, vegetables and gravy into a 2 pint (1¼ litre) greased ovenproof dish.
5. To make crumble, sift flour, mustard and salt into a bowl. Rub in butter or margarine finely. Toss in thyme.
6. Sprinkle crumble thickly over beef mixture then reheat and brown for 30 minutes just above oven centre set to 200°C (400°F), Gas 6. Serve piping hot with green vegetables to taste.

Barley Beef with Brown Crumble *Serves 4*

Make as above but coat meat with only 1oz (25g) flour and add 2oz (50g) pearl barley to the stew while it is simmering. Use brown flour for the crumble instead of white.

Mixed Meat Goulash *Serves 4*

A beef and pork mixture combine to make a traditional-type Goulash which virtually cooks in its own juices. For the most apt accompaniment, choose small pasta. No additional vegetables are required as they have already been built in to the Goulash.

3oz (75g) lard (to be traditional) or margarine
8oz (225g) onions, peeled and chopped
2 garlic cloves, peeled and crushed
2 medium green peppers, washed and dried
1½lb (675g) equal amounts stewing pork and braising steak, washed and cubed
1½ level tblsp paprika
8oz (225g) blanched tomatoes, skinned and chopped
1½ level tsp salt
1 level tsp caraway seeds, optional
1 carton (5oz or 142ml) soured cream

1. Heat lard or margarine in saucepan until hot and sizzling. Add onions, garlic and peppers. Fry over a medium heat until pale gold.
2. Move to edges of pan then dry meats thoroughly. Add to pan and fry briskly until well-sealed, turning frequently.
3. Stir in paprika, tomatoes, salt and caraway seeds. Bring to boil, lower heat and cover.
4. Simmer 1½ to 2 hours or until meats are tender, stirring occasionally. Whisk in soured cream and serve very hot.

Beef in the Stroganov Style

Serves 4

This could be called elaborate with its rump steak and cream, and therefore it is best kept for special occasions and mini celebrations — or for those times when you are just feeling extravagant!

1lb (450g) rump steak (weight *after* all fat has been removed)
2oz (50g) butter
4oz (125g) onion, peeled and finely grated
2 level tblsp tubed or canned tomato purée
¼pt (150ml) double cream
1oz (25g) pickled cucumber, very finely chopped

salt and pepper to taste
freshly cooked rice for serving, allowing about 1½oz (40g) per
  person

1. Cut steak into narrow strips, about 3 ins (7½cm) in length,
   making sure you slice *against* the grain of the meat.
2. Melt butter in fairly large frying pan then add onion. Cover
   with lid or inverted enamel plate and fry gently for about 10
   minutes or until onion softens but stays white.
3. Increase heat and fry steaks, a heaped tablespoon at a time,
   in the pan until cooked; about 5 to 6 minutes.
4. Stir in purée and cream then bring just up to the boil.
   Remove from heat and stir in cucumber. Season to taste with
   salt and pepper.
5. Spoon rice on to individual plates and spoon over the
   Stroganov. Eat straight away.

Belgian Beef in Beer   *Serves 6*

Very much a Belgian national dish, and a fantasy of mellow
flavours, cleverly woven together into a memorable culinary
tapestry.

2oz (50g) margarine
12oz (350g) onions, peeled and chopped
2lb (450g) chuck steak, washed and dried then cut into smallish
  cubes
1oz (25g) flour
¾pt (425ml) lager
2 level tsp salt
1 level tblsp dark brown soft sugar
2 tsp malt vinegar
1 bouquet garni bag
3 large slices brown bread, decrusted
1½ rounded tsp French mustard

127

1. Heat margarine in a pan. Add onions. Fry over medium heat until pale gold. Meanwhile toss beef cubes in flour.
2. Move onions to edges of pan and add beef. Fry briskly until well-sealed and brown.
3. Mix in lager, salt, sugar, vinegar, bouquet garni bag and any leftover flour.
4. Bring to boil, stirring. Lower heat and cover pan. Simmer 1½ to 2 hours or until beef is tender.
5. To thicken, spread bread with mustard, cut into large cubes and add to the beef. Stir until bread has completely broken down and turns into coarse crumbs.
6. Remove bouquet garni bag then serve straight away with boiled potatoes and cooked green vegetables to taste.

Stout Beef

Serves 6

As we are blessed with Guinness and barley wine, I usually adapt the recipe above by using stout instead of lager, and including 1 peeled and crushed garlic clove with 6oz (175g) skinned tomatoes.

Stylish Beef

Serves 6 to 7

A pot roast with panache from the French culinary stables.

3lb (1½kg) braising steak, in one piece
1½oz (40g) flour
2oz (50g) margarine
¾pt (425ml) dry red wine
1 garlic clove, peeled and crushed
6 smallish whole onions, peeled
6 medium-sized whole carrots, peeled

1 bouquet garni bag
2 level tsp salt
pepper to taste
8oz (225g) trimmed and washed mushrooms, thinly sliced
1 liqueur glass brandy

1. Wash and dry steak and coat all over with flour, pressing it well into all cracks and crevices.
2. Heat margarine in large pan until sizzling. Add beef and fry briskly all over until well-browned. Remove to a plate temporarily.
3. Pour wine into pan then add garlic, whole onions, whole carrots and the bouquet garni bag. Bring to the boil and replace meat plus any leftover flour. Season with salt and pepper.
4. Cover. Simmer very gently for 2½ to 3 hours or until meat is tender, stirring occasionally. Add mushrooms, mix in well and continue to cook a further ½ hour. Remove bouquet garni bag.
5. Transfer meat to a board and carve into slices. Arrange on a warm dish, coat with gravy then surround with vegetables. Accompany with whole boiled potatoes and a green salad.

Pot-Roasted Cider Beef   *Serves 6 to 7*

Make exactly as above but use dry cider instead of stock and add 2 peeled, quartered and cored dessert apples at the same time as the mushrooms.

Boeuf Bourguignonne   *Serves 4 to 6*

That very special beef stew from France which finds its way on to the menus of top hotels and restaurants.

2oz (50g) butter or margarine
1 tblsp salad oil
8oz (225g) onions, peeled and chopped
1 garlic clove, peeled and crushed
6oz (175g) gammon, chopped
2lb (900g) cubed braising steak, washed and dried
3 level tblsp flour
¾pt (425ml) dry red wine
1 bouquet garni bag
1 level tsp salt
4oz (125g) trimmed button mushrooms
pepper to taste
2 heaped tblsp chopped parsley

1. Heat butter or margarine and salad oil in a pan. Add onions, garlic and gammon and fry over a medium heat until pale gold.
2. Mix in steak and fry a little more briskly until well-sealed and golden brown.
3. Stir in flour and cook 2 minutes, turning meat over and over all the time.
4. Gradually blend in wine then add bouquet garni bag and salt.

Bring to boil, stirring. Lower heat and cover. Simmer 2 to 2½ hours or until meat is tender. Stir occasionally.

5. Remove bouquet garni bag, add mushrooms and pepper to taste, then cook for a further 15 minutes.
6. Transfer to a warm dish and sprinkle with parsley. Accompany with boiled potatoes and green vegetables to taste.

Kidneys 'en Chemise'

Serves 4

A pleasing idea for lambs' kidneys and highly acceptable served on slices of butter-fried bread or 4 ins (10cm) squares of freshly baked puff pastry.

8 lambs' kidneys
3oz (75g) fresh brown breadcrumbs
2oz (50g) onion, peeled and grated
1 slightly rounded tblsp finely-chopped parsley
½ level tsp marjoram
1 level tsp finely-grated lemon peel
½ level tsp powder mustard
pepper to taste
beaten egg to bind
8 *long* rashers streaky bacon, de-rinded if necessary
mayonnaise

1. 'Peel' kidneys by removing the thin, natural film casing around each. Wash and dry.
2. For stuffing, tip crumbs into a mixing bowl. Toss in onion, parsley, marjoram, lemon peel, mustard and pepper to taste.
3. Bind with beaten egg, (depending on size of egg, you may have to add a little milk to hold stuffing together) then spread over bacon rashers.
4. Wrap round kidneys and secure with wooden cocktail sticks.
5. Transfer to a lightly greased small roasting tin and cook 25 minutes in centre of oven set to 190°C (375°F), Gas 5. When

ready, the bacon should be crisp and golden and the kidneys cooked through.

6. Remove sticks and place kidneys 'en chemise' on to 4 slices of freshly fried bread or pastry squares. Top each with 2 teaspoons mayonnaise and serve straight away.

Chicken Livers De-Luxe
Serves 4 to 6

With tubs of frozen chicken livers so readily available from supermarket chains and freezer centres, it makes sense to use them in this rich and creamy main course as a midweek special. The idea comes from North America.

2 tubs (1lb or 450g) chicken livers
2 level tblsp flour
1½oz (40g) butter or margarine
4oz (125g) onion, peeled and finely chopped
3 tblsp white port
3 tblsp water
1 to 1½ level tsp salt
1 carton (5oz or 142ml) soured cream
3 slightly rounded tblsp salad cream
paprika
1 medium ripe avocado
lemon juice

1. Wash and dry chicken livers then coat all over with flour.
2. Heat butter or margarine in frying pan. Add onion and fry until light gold.
3. Mix in livers and continue to fry until well-browned. Add port, water and salt. Stir well to mix then cover pan and simmer gently until livers are cooked through; about 20 to 25 minutes.
4. Stir from time to time to prevent sticking then lift livers out

of pan into a warm dish. Add the soured cream and salad cream to juices left in pan.

5. Heat through briefly until hot. Pour over livers then sprinkle with paprika. Garnish with dice of peeled avocado, sprinkled with lemon juice to prevent browning.

Saucy Liver Casserole

Serves 4

A fried liver and vegetable mix, topped with zesty mustard sauce then casseroled in the oven.

A saucy liver

1lb (450g) pork or lamb's liver, very thinly sliced
1oz (25g) margarine
3oz (25g) streaky bacon, chopped
3oz (75g) onion, peeled and chopped
3oz (75g) trimmed and washed mushrooms, sliced

Sauce
1oz (25g) butter or margarine
1oz (25g) flour
¼pt (150ml) beef stock (use cube and water)
¼pt (150ml) water
1 heaped tblsp scissor-snipped chives
1 heaped tblsp finely-chopped parsley
½ level tsp finely-grated lemon peel
1 tsp Worcester sauce
3 level tsp prepared continental mustard
1 level tsp salt
pepper to taste

1. Wash and dry liver and use to cover base of 2 pint (1¼ litre) ovenproof dish.
2. Heat margarine and bacon until sizzling. Add onion and fry over a medium heat until golden brown. Mix in mushrooms. Fry a further 5 minutes.
3. Spread over liver and leave on one side temporarily while making sauce.
4. Melt butter or margarine in a saucepan. Stir in flour to form a roux. Gradually blend in beef stock and water.
5. Cook, stirring continuously, until mixture comes to the boil and thickens. Add all remaining ingredients.
6. Pour over liver and vegetables in dish. Cover with lid or foil and cook 40 minutes in oven centre set to 180°C (350°F), Gas 4. Serve with creamed potatoes and sprouts.

Liver and Mushroom Pie

Serves 4

A full-of-flavour pie packed with liver and vegetables.

1lb (450g) ox liver, cubed and soaked 1 hour in milk to reduce
   bitterness
salt and pepper to taste
1oz (25g) flour
1oz (25g) butter or margarine
3oz (75g) streaky bacon, chopped
4oz (125g) onions, peeled and chopped
4oz (125g) mushrooms, trimmed then washed and sliced
¼pt (150ml) water
6oz (175g) shortcrust pastry made with 6oz (175g) flour and 3oz
   (75g) fat etc
beaten egg for brushing

1. Wash and dry liver then season to taste with salt and pepper.
   Coat with flour.
2. Heat butter or margarine in pan. Add bacon and fry over
   medium heat until fat runs and bacon becomes crispy.
3. Move to edge of pan then add liver and onions. Fry fairly
   briskly until both turn a warm gold.
4. Mix in mushrooms and water then bring to boil and adjust
   seasoning to taste. Lower heat. Cover pan.
5. Simmer about 1 hour or until liver is tender, stirring
   occasionally. Cool completely. Spoon into a 1½ pint (1 litre)
   well-greased pie dish with rim.
6. For lid, roll out pastry 1 in (2½cm) larger all the way round
   than top of dish.
7. Moisten edges with water, line with pastry strips cut from
   trimmings and brush with more water. Cover with pastry lid
   and press edges of lining strips and lid together to seal. Trim.
8. Brush with egg then decorate with pastry leaves, rolled and
   cut from remainder of trimmings. Brush with more egg.
9. Bake 25 minutes just above oven centre set to 220°C (425°F),
   Gas 7. Serve hot with green vegetables.

Desserts

OK — so sweets and puddings are not your strong point. Your soufflés collapse, your pancakes are leathery and your pastry a nightmare. You'd like to create gorgeous concoctions which would amaze your family and have your guests gasping with admiration — look no further. Here are recipes for desserts of all kinds, from the ridiculously easy to the elaborately lavish; glorious puds that will ensure you will never have to say, 'I can't cook desserts,' again.

My Best Cheesecake

Serves 10

Gloriously rich but smooth as silk is the best way of describing my favourite Cheesecake which I have been making for years.

4oz (125g) digestive biscuits, crushed
1 level tsp cinnamon
1oz (25g) light brown soft sugar
1½lb (675g) cream cheese, at kitchen temperature and softened
1½oz (40g) cornflour
5oz (125g) caster sugar
3 Grade 3 eggs, beaten
1tsp vanilla essence
finely-grated peel and juice of 1 large washed and dried lemon
¼pt (150ml) double cream, whipped until thick

1. Mix digestive biscuits with cinnamon and brown sugar. Spread fairly thickly over base of 10 ins (25cm) spring clip tin, well-greased with butter.
2. Beat cream cheese until absolutely smooth with cornflour, caster sugar, eggs, vanilla essence and grated peel and juice of the lemon. Alternatively, mix in blender or food processor then spoon into a mixing bowl.
3. Gently whisk in cream then spread mixture evenly into prepared tin. Bake 45 minutes in oven centre set to 150°C (300°F), Gas 2. Switch oven heat off, open door and leave cake in oven until lukewarm.
4. Take out of oven and leave until cold before unclipping sides. Leave on metal base for serving.

Fruit-Topped Cheesecake

Serves 10

Cover cold cheesecake with 1 can fruit pie filling, flavour to taste.

Cream-Topped Cheesecake   *Serves 10*

Spread lukewarm cake with 1 carton (5oz or 142ml) soured cream.

Coupe Angelike   *Serves 4*

An impressive sweet for a dinner party. If numbers are larger than four, double or even treble the ingredients.

4 canned pineapple rings (large)
6 tblsp Tia Maria
4 choc ices (vanilla ice cream bars covered with chocolate coating)
¼pt (150ml) double cream
1 level tsp drinking chocolate

1. Cut pineapple rings into small pieces and put into a mixing bowl. Toss with 4 tablespoons Tia Maria then divide between 4 glasses.
2. Cut choc ices into cubes and spoon equal amounts into glasses over fruit.
3. Whip cream until thick with remaining Tia Maria. Dollop into glasses and dust each with drinking chocolate. Serve straight away.

Coupe Manhatten   *Serves 4*

One of my own cooling ideas with a modern, cocktail look.

Divide 1 can grapefruit segments in syrup between 4 tall glasses. Two-thirds fill with Raspberry Sorbet (page 146) then trickle

Cassis over each. Decorate with fresh mint leaves and serve straight away. If mint leaves are unavailable, decorate each with a thin slice of unpeeled cucumber.

Lime Clouds

Serves 4

The foundation is nothing more elaborate and demanding than a simple semolina pudding. Then come the frills . . .!

1pt (575ml) milk
2oz (50g) semolina
2oz (50g) caster sugar
finely-grated peel and juice of 1 washed and dried lime
2 Grade 3 eggs, separated

1. Pour milk into a saucepan. Shower in the semolina. Bring to boil, stirring constantly until mixture thickens. Simmer 3 minutes then stir in sugar, half the lime peel, all the juice and the egg yolks.
2. Mix thoroughly then set aside for the moment. Whisk egg whites to a stiff snow and beat one-third gently into the semolina mixture.
3. Fold in rest of whites with a large metal spoon then, when smooth and evenly-combined, spoon into 4 dishes. Sprinkle tops with remaining lime peel and leave until cold.
4. Chill in the refrigerator at least 1 hour before serving.

Chocolate Clouds

Serves 4

Make exactly as above but add 3½oz (100g) melted plain chocolate to the milk with semolina. Omit lime and flavour with

1 level teaspoon vanilla essence. Sprinkle with chocolate vermicelli.

Foaming Peach Melbas   *Serves 6*

A new twist to an old theme — jellied Peach Melba with its somewhat mousse-like character and daisy fresh raspberry sauce.

1 lemon flavour jelly, divided into cubes
cold water
6 canned peach halves, well-drained
3 tsp lemon juice
¼pt (150ml) vanilla ice cream, softened
2 Grade 2 egg whites

Sauce
8oz (225g) fresh raspberries
2oz (50g) icing sugar, sifted
1 tblsp Kirsch or cherry brandy

1. Put jelly into a measuring cup and make up to ½ pint (275ml) with water.
2. Tip into a saucepan and melt, stirring, over a low heat. Blend peach halves and lemon juice to a smooth purée in blender or food processor.
3. Add to jelly, mix thoroughly and leave until completely cold. Beat in the softened ice cream.
4. Whisk egg whites to a stiff snow. Beat one-third into the jelly mixture then fold in remainder with a large metal spoon.
5. When smooth and evenly combined, pour into 6 sundae glasses. Set in the refrigerator.
6. For sauce, crush raspberries finely then stir in sugar and Kirsch or cherry brandy. Spoon over Melbas just before serving.

Foaming Pear Melbas

Serves 6

Make as above, using 8 canned and well-drained pear halves instead of the peaches.

Red Wine Jelly

Serves 8

Made for high days and holidays in Victorian times and still enjoyed widely in Northern Europe, this is my adaptation of a recipe found in a turn of the century encyclopaedia.

2 envelopes or 6 level tsp gelatine
¼pt (150ml) cold water
1 litre bottle (1¾pt) red wine (*not* plonk)
thinly-cut peel from 1 medium washed and dried lemon
thinly-cut peel from 1 medium washed and dried orange
4 cloves
1 blade of mace or ½ level tsp nutmeg
3 ins (7½cm) piece of cinnamon stick
caster sugar to taste
single cream

1. Mix together gelatine and cold water and leave aside for time being.
2. Pour wine into pan with fruit peels, cloves, mace or nutmeg and the cinnamon stick. Heat until hot but not boiling. Sweeten to taste. Cover. Leave until lukewarm so that flavours have a chance to blend together.
3. Strain into clean bowl. Take out 5 tablespoons and put into small saucepan. Add gelatine. Stir over minimal heat until gelatine dissolves but do not allow to boil.
4. Combine with rest of spiced wine then pour into 8 bowls or glasses. Refrigerate until firm. Pour cream over each.

Golden Wine Jelly with Cherry Cream

Serves 8

Not very often made but quite exquisite with sweet white wine and mint leaves for flavouring.

Make as above but heat white wine with the thinly-cut peel from orange and 8 medium mint leaves. Sweeten to taste with clear honey. When set, top each with ¼pt (150ml) double cream whipped until thick, flavoured with 1oz (25g) chopped maraschino cherries and sweetened to taste with caster sugar.

Note
For 4 portions, halve all the ingredients.

Campari Peaches

Serves 4

For devotees of Campari, what better dessert than peaches steeped in a Campari marinade and served with Kiwi sorbet.

4½oz (140g) caster sugar
9 tblsp water
4 tblsp grenadine syrup
2 tblsp Campari
4 large and ripe peaches, blanched as tomatoes then skinned and halved
1 tblsp lemon juice

1. Put sugar, water, grenadine syrup and Campari into a saucepan. Stir over a low heat until sugar dissolves.
2. Bring to the boil and boil for 2 minutes. Pour into a shallow mixing bowl.
3. Brush peach halves with lemon juice and add to bowl. Baste with Campari liquid and leave, covered, in the refrigerator for a minimum of 4 hours or until well chilled.
4. Put 2 tablespoons of Kiwi Sorbet (page 146) into each of 4 sundae glasses. Top with peaches and Campari syrup. Serve straight away.

Note
For winter eating, well-drained canned peach halves may be used.

Kissel

Serves 8

A lightly set fruit 'blancmange' which is eaten in Scandinavia, Northern Europe and the Soviet Union. It can be made from any combination of red fruits and is heaven on a summer's day.

2pt (1¼ litre) strained fruit juice made from cooking red berry
   fruits, currants and/or cherries in water with no sugar
9oz (250g) granulated sugar
finely-grated peel of a small washed and dried lemon
3oz (75g) potato flour or arrowroot
4 tblsp cold water
extra caster sugar
¼pt (150ml) single cream

1. Put fruit juice, sugar and lemon peel into a pan. Heat slowly
   until sugar dissolves.
2. Mix potato flour or arrowroot with water. Pour into fruit
   juice mixture and bring to boil, stirring all the time.
3. Simmer 3 minutes, spoon into 8 bowls (not crystal or they
   might crack with the heat) and sprinkle with sugar to prevent
   a skin from forming.
4. Leave until lukewarm then refrigerate several hours until
   cold and set. Float cream on top of each before serving.

Gooseberry and Rhubarb Kissel

Serves 8

Prepare as above, using only topped and tailed gooseberries
and chopped-up rhubarb to make the juice.

Strawberry Sorbet

Serves 8

Cool as ice and tingling fresh, homemade sorbets retain a
fabulous fruit bouquet and make a fine finish to a top class
meal.

8oz (225g) strawberries, washed and hulled
2 tblsp Kirsch
4oz (125g) caster sugar
red food colouring
1 Grade 2 egg white

1. Blend strawberries, with Kirsch and sugar, to a smooth purée in blender goblet or food processor.
2. Tip into bowl and heighten colour of strawberries by mixing in a few drops of red food colouring.
3. Cover and leave in deep freeze 1½ to 2 hours or until mixture has frozen about 2 ins (5cm) round edges of dish.
4. Tip into a second bowl, beat gently to break down ice crystals then whisk until fruit mixture is light and aerated.
5. Wash beaters then whisk egg white to a stiff snow. Fold into strawberry mixture.
6. Cover again and freeze several hours or until firm. Before serving, leave to soften 20 to 30 minutes at kitchen temperature then spoon into small dishes. Serve at once as sorbet melts quickly.

Raspberry Sorbet   *Serves 8*

Make exactly as above but use raspberries instead of strawberries and orange liqueur instead of Kirsch.

Kiwi Fruit Sorbet   *Serves 8*

Make exactly as Strawberry Sorbet but use 5 peeled and sliced Kiwi fruit instead of strawberries and apricot brandy instead of Kirsch. Heighten colour with green food colouring.

Strawberries Romanoff

Serves 4

A grand old Russian-style dessert which was much favoured in Court circles.

1lb (450g) strawberries
4 tblsp Curaçao
¼pt (150ml) double cream
1½oz (40g) caster sugar

1. Wash strawberries gently and wipe dry with kitchen paper. Reserve 4 of the best for decoration. Hull remainder and slice.
2. Put into a mixing bowl and toss with Curaçao. Cover and chill in the refrigerator for 2 hours.
3. Before serving, whip cream until thick then gently fold in sugar.
4. Spoon strawberries and liqueur into glasses then pile whipped cream on top. Decorate each with a whole strawberry.

Strawberries Romanoff in Pineapple

Serves 4 generously

Make strawberry mixture as above. After mixing with Curaçao and chilling for 2 hours, fold into the whipped cream. Halve 2 small pineapples lengthwise and cut out centre cores. Pile with strawberry mixture and decorate with whole strawberries.

Pavlova

Serves about 8

With roots 'down-under' in Australia and New Zealand, Pavlova

With roots 'down-under'

is a whoosh of crispy-on-the-outside and soft-in-the-middle meringue, happy as can be with a filling of cream or ice cream and all manner of fruits.

3 Grade 2 egg whites
½ tsp lemon juice
7½oz (215g) caster sugar
1 tsp vinegar
3 level tsp cornflour
½pt (275ml) double cream, whipped and sweetened to taste

1. Line a baking tray with Bakewell non-stick parchment paper. Outline an 8 ins (20cm) circle on top. Under *no circumstances* brush with fat or Pavlova will stick.
2. Tip egg whites into a bowl. Add lemon juice and whisk to a stiff snow. Add two-thirds of the sugar and continue to whisk until meringue is shiny and stands in tall, firm peaks when beaters are lifted out of bowl.
3. Fold in rest of sugar with vinegar and cornflour. Spoon thickly on to prepared tray, completely filling in marked circle.
4. Smooth top with knife dipped in and out of water then bake 1 hour in oven centre set to 150°C (300°F), Gas 2.
5. Turn out carefully on to a flat plate and gently ease away paper. Leave the Pavlova to cool upside down (which is actually the right way up!) and, as it does so, it might sink slightly in the centre to form a hollow. Fill with cream, stud with strawberries or raspberries and cut into portions.

Ice Cream Pavlova   *Serves about 8*

Fill with vanilla ice cream then stud with berry fruit.

New Zealand Pavlova

Serves about 8

Make as the cream-filled Pavlova then cover top completely with peeled and sliced Kiwi fruit.

Tropical Pavlova

Serves about 8

Make as cream-filled Pavlova but fill with sweetened whipped cream to which ½oz (15g) toasted coconut has been added. Top with pieces of canned pineapple and lychees then dot here and there with slices of preserved ginger, first well-drained.

Rose Syllabub

Serves 4

Made with rosé wine, this Syllabub turns more pink than usual and is fit for any important occasion.

¼pt (150ml) rosé wine
finely-grated peel and strained juice of 1 medium lemon
3oz (75g) caster sugar
½pt (275ml) double cream

1. Pour wine into bowl and stir in lemon peel, juice and sugar. Cover and refrigerate a minimum of 4 hours until mixture is thoroughly chilled.
2. Add cream then beat steadily, preferably with electric beaters, until mixture thickens and forms soft peaks.
3. Spoon into 4 glasses and chill overnight before serving.

Cider Syllabub

Serves 4

Make exactly as Rosé Syllabub, using medium cider instead of rosé wine.

White Wine Syllabub

Serves 4

Make exactly as Rosé Syllabub, using a sweetish white wine instead of rosé wine.

Mandarin Syllabub

Serves 6

Divide 1 can of mandarins and their syrup evenly between 6 glasses. Spoon any of the above syllabub mixtures over each and sprinkle with 3 level teaspoons chopped pistachio nuts or walnuts.

Instant Peach Pudding

Serves 6

One I like, in that it can be put together in a matter of minutes and still look impressive.

6 thick slices jam-filled Swiss roll
3 tblsp sweet sherry
6 canned peach halves, drained (keep syrup for drinks, sauces, etc)
¼pt (150ml) double cream
1oz (25g) caster sugar
1 slightly rounded tblsp black cherry jam

151

1. Place slices of Swiss roll on 6 individual plates. Moisten with sherry.
2. Stand a peach half on each, cut sides uppermost.
3. Whip cream until thick. Stir in sugar. Pile into peach cavities then decorate with jam.

Mock Poires Belle Hélène   *Serves 6*

Really for cheats, this falls into the bracket of the recipe above for its 'instant' success rating.

Put 6 thick slices of chocolate Swiss roll on to individual plates and moisten with syrup from can of pears. Top each slice with a pear half, cut side uppermost. Fill cavities generously with vanilla ice cream then trickle shop-bought chocolate sauce over each.

Autumn Compôte   *Serves 8*
with Grand Marnier

A smart compôte, this one, and very suitable for a dinner party.

1lb (450g) washed cooking plums, halved and stoned

1lb (450g) peeled cooking apples, quartered then cored and sliced

¼pt (150ml) water

finely-grated peel and juice of 1 medium orange

6oz (175g) granulated sugar

4 tblsp Grand Marnier

1. Put fruits into a pan with water. Add water, orange peel and sugar.
2. Cook gently, stirring occasionally, until fruit is just soft but do not allow it to overcook and break up.
3. Remove from heat. Cool completely. Cover. Refrigerate several hours or until well chilled. Stir in Grand Marnier just before serving. Accompany with sponge fingers.

Grape and Banana Salad   *Serves 6*

A simple yet subtle fruit salad laced with mead and garnished with toasted pine nuts.

8oz (225g) black grapes, washed and dried

8oz (225g) green grapes, washed and dried

4 tblsp mead

2 tblsp lemon juice

3 large bananas

1oz (25g) pine nuts, lightly toasted

1. Halve grapes and remove seeds. Put into bowl. Add mead and lemon juice.
2. Cover. Chill in the refrigerator about 2 hours. Before serving, slice in bananas and mix well.
3. Spoon into 6 dishes and sprinkle each with nuts.

Italian Brandy Oranges

Serves 8

Because the preparation is fairly slow, I would suggest you make these for special occasions, using half as many ingredients for four people and doubling them for sixteen.

8 large oranges, washed and dried
8oz (225g) caster sugar
½pt (275ml) water
2 tblsp brandy

1. Peel oranges *very thinly,* reserving the peel from 3. Cut reserved peel into slim strips and put into saucepan. Cover with water. Bring to boil and lower heat. Cover. Simmer gently for ¼ hour. Drain thoroughly and keep peel aside.
2. Remove all traces of white pith from the oranges. Put sugar and water into a clean pan and stir over a low heat until sugar dissolves.
3. Bring to boil and boil steadily for a few minutes or until mixture becomes syrupy. Do not allow it to turn colour so watch carefully as sugar liquids turn golden fairly rapidly. Also do not stir and keep pan uncovered.
4. Cool to lukewarm and stir in brandy. Add oranges, one at a time, and toss over and over in the syrup. Lift out of pan with a perforated spoon or fish slice and put into a shallow serving bowl.
5. Add orange peel strips to remaining syrup in pan. Cook slowly, uncovered, until the peel looks transparent and the syrup becomes deep golden in colour.
6. Strain syrup over oranges then top each with orange peel. Leave until completely cold before serving and provide knives and forks as oranges are difficult to eat otherwise.

Danish Apple 'Cake' *Serves 4*

Not so much a cake in the traditional sense but a multi-layered build-up of puréed apples and sweetened buttery crumbs, topped with cream and decorated with jam.

1½lb (675g) peeled cooking apples, cored and thinly sliced
3 tblsp water
6oz (175g) caster sugar
3oz (75g) butter
3oz (75g) fresh white breadcrumbs
2oz (50g) light brown soft sugar
1 level tsp cinnamon

Topping
¼pt (150ml) double cream
1 tblsp cold milk
1 level tblsp caster sugar
4 tsp plum jam

1. Put apples into pan with water. Bring to boil, lower heat and cover. Simmer over low heat until apples become soft and pulpy.
2. Beat until smooth, add sugar and continue to whisk over a low heat until sugar dissolves completely. Tip into basin and leave until cold.
3. For crumb mixture, melt butter in a clean pan. Add crumbs and fry until lightly browned, stirring frequently. Mix in sugar and cinnamon then cool completely.
4. Before serving, whisk cream and milk together until thick. Stir in sugar.
5. To assemble, fill 4 tumblers with alternate layers of apple and crumb mixture, finishing with a layer of crumbs.
6. Top each with mounds of whipped cream then add a teaspoon of jam. Refrigerate about 45 minutes before serving.

Peasant Girl with Veil

Serves 4

Another Danish speciality, this one is made exactly as the above recipe but the breadcrumbs are made from mid-brown rye bread, Danish for preference.

Apple and Raspberry 'Cake'

As an alternative, mix the apple purée with 1 tblsp of lemon juice and add a layer of tinned raspberries (drained) to the apple purée and breadcrumb layers. Top with whipped cream and decorate with a few reserved raspberries instead of the jam.

Strawberries and Cream Junket

Serves 4

Very English, very tea-on-the-lawn and also a super luxury sweet for those who still remember junket as a treat.

1pt (575ml) milk (not long life)
1 level tblsp caster sugar
1 tsp vanilla essence
1 tsp rennet essence
8oz (225g) fresh strawberries
icing sugar to taste
clotted cream

1. Pour milk in a pan. Add sugar. Stir over a low heat until sugar dissolves and mixture reaches blood heat. To test, dip the tip of your little finger into the milk and it should strike

neither hot nor cold — just tepid.
2. Remove from heat then stir in vanilla essence and rennet. Mix gently round with a spoon.
3. Pour into 4 bowls or dishes, leaving a 1 in (2½cm) gap at the top of each. Cover each then leave at kitchen temperature until set.
4. Transfer to the refrigerator and chill about 3 hours. Before serving, crush strawberries and spoon gently on top of each bowl of junket. Pass the cream separately.

Raspberries and Cream Junket   *Serves 4*

Make as above, substituting 6oz (175g) raspberries for strawberries.

Cranberry and Orange Creams   *Serves 4*

Based on a Scandinavian idea, this is a glowing and tangy sweet, its richness tempered by the addition of cranberry sauce, orange peel and egg white.

½pt (275ml) double cream
3 tblsp milk
4 well-rounded tblsp cranberry sauce
1 level tsp finely-grated orange peel
2 egg whites from Grade 3 eggs
¼ tsp lemon juice

1. Whip cream and milk together until thick. Gently fold in cranberry sauce and orange peel with a metal spoon.
2. Beat egg whites to a stiff snow with lemon juice. Whip one-third gently into the cream and cranberry mixture.
3. Lightly fold in rest of egg whites then pile mixture into 4 dishes. Refrigerate at least 1 hour before serving.

Black Forest Cherry Cake   *Serves 8 to 10*

Few desserts have reached the top of the popularity charts as quickly as this Black Forest import and although many recipes are to be found all over Germany and here as well, this is a fairly uncluttered version though it, too, is quite time-consuming to make.

5oz (150g) self-raising flour
1oz (25g) cocoa powder
1½oz (40g) cornflour
6oz (175g) butter or block margarine, at kitchen temperature
6oz (175g) caster sugar
1 tsp vanilla essence
3 Grade 3 eggs, at kitchen temperature

Filling
1 can or jar (about 13½oz or 385g) cherry pie filling

4 tblsp Kirsch or cherry brandy
¾pt (425ml) double cream
¼pt (150ml) single cream
2oz (50g) caster sugar

Decoration
chocolate vermicelli
6 glacé cherries, halved

1. To make cake, grease and base-line 2 × 8 ins (20cm) sandwich tins with greaseproof paper. Set oven to 180°C (350°F), Gas 4.
2. Sift flour, cocoa and cornflour on to a plate. Cream butter or margarine and sugar together until light and fluffy. Add the vanilla essence then beat in eggs individually, adding a heaped tablespoon of sifted dry ingredients with each. Fold in rest of dry ingredients.
3. Spread evenly into tins and bake 25 to 30 minutes in oven centre. Turn out on to wire cooling racks and peel away paper. When completely cold, cut each through horizontally.
4. Mix cherry pie filling with half the Kirsch or cherry brandy. Whip creams together until thick then sweeten with sugar by folding in gently. Gently stir in rest of alcohol.
5. Sandwich cake layers together with all the cherry pie filling mixture and just over one-third of cream.
6. Spread rest of cream over top and sides of cake then press chocolate vermicelli against sides. Decorate with halved cherries. Chill lightly in the refrigerator before serving.

Grape Brulée
Serves 4

A lighter, fruit-based version of Crème Brulée.

1lb (450g) grapes, washed and dried
2 level tblsp clear honey
½pt (275ml) double cream, whipped
3oz (55g) soft brown sugar

1. Halve the grapes and remove pips. Place in ovenproof dish or 4 individual dishes, reserving some grapes for decoration. Coat evenly with honey.
2. Spoon the whipped cream over the grapes, then refrigerate a minimum of 3 hours. Before serving, cover cream completely by sprinkling thickly with the sugar.
3. Grill under a pre-heated, very hot grill until the sugar caramelises. When cool, decorate with the reserved grapes.

Mocha Cream Mousse with Pears

Serves 4

Unashamedly rich, exquisitely-flavoured and the perfect ending to a memorable meal. Two variations follow:

1 can (about 1lb or 450g) pears, drained
1 bar (3½oz or 100g) plain chocolate
½oz (15g) butter
4 Grade 2 eggs, kitchen temperature and separated
4 tsp coffee liqueur
¼pt (150ml) double cream

1. Chop pears and divide equally between 4 *large,* wine-type glasses.
2. Break up chocolate and put, with butter, into bowl standing over pan of hot water. Leave until melted, stirring once or twice.
3. Remove basin from pan and wipe sides dry. Add egg yolks and coffee liqueur to chocolate mixture and beat in well.
4. Whisk egg whites to a stiff snow in clean and dry bowl. Beat one-third into chocolate mixture then fold in remainder with a large metal spoon.
5. Spoon over pears and tap lightly so that tops are level. Chill at least 6 hours in the refrigerator. Before serving, float unwhipped cream on top.

Chocolate Cherry Cream Mousse

Serves 4

Make as recipe above but use 1 can drained cherries instead of pears. Flavour chocolate mixture with 4 teaspoons cherry brandy.

Chocolate Mandarin Cream Mousse

Serves 4

Make as first recipe but use 1 can drained mandarins instead of pears. Flavour chocolate mixture with 4 teaspoons orange-flavoured liqueur.

Note
Keep drained syrups for drinks, for adding to trifles and for sweetening stewed fruit.

Strawberry Apple Chantilly

Serves 6

One of those rich, elegant desserts which tastes luxurious yet is surprisingly trouble-free to make.

2lb (900g) peeled and quartered cooking apples, cored and
   sliced
5 tblsp water
5 tblsp granulated sugar
1 level tsp cinnamon
2 slightly-rounded tblsp strawberry jam
¼pt (150ml) double cream
1 tblsp cold milk
extra cinnamon

1. Put apple slices into a pan. Add water and bring to boil. Lower heat and cover. Cook over a medium heat until they turn very soft and pulpy.
2. Beat until smooth. Add sugar and stir until dissolved. Mix in cinnamon and jam. Leave until completely cold.
3. Beat cream and milk together until thick. Gently fold into apple mixture with a large metal spoon.
4. Transfer to 6 glasses or dishes and sprinkle lightly with cinnamon. Chill at least 1 hour in the refrigerator before serving.

Froth O' Fruit

Serves 8

A sophisticated sweet, swiftly made when time is precious.

1 can (about 14oz or 400g) raspberry fruit pie filling
1 can (about 14oz or 400g) cherry fruit pie filling
4 Grade 3 eggs, separated
1 level tsp finely-grated lemon peel
½ tsp lemon juice

1. Spoon fruit pie fillings, together, into large pan. Warm slowly, stirring, until bubbly and hot.
2. Remove from heat and stir in egg yolks and lemon peel. Leave aside temporarily.
3. In clean and dry bowl, beat egg whites and lemon juice to a stiff snow. Using a large metal spoon, gently and lightly fold into fruit mixture.
4. When smooth and evenly-combined, spoon into 8 large, wine-type glasses. Chill in the refrigerator at least 1 hour before serving. Accompany with crisp biscuits.

Advocaat Cream Flakes

Serves 6

Another alcoholic contribution, this time based on cream and apricots.

1 can (15oz or 425g) apricots, drained
2 tblsp brandy (or apricot brandy if you have any in stock)
½pt (275ml) double cream
2 tblsp milk
4 tblsp Advocaat
2oz (50g) flaked almonds, lightly toasted

1. Divide apricots between 6 bowls and sprinkle brandy or apricot brandy over each.
2. Whip cream and milk together until thick. Gently fold in Advocaat. Spoon over apricots.
3. Sprinkle with almonds then chill in the refrigerator for about 2 to 3 hours.

Note
Keep syrup for drinks.

Chestnut Cream with Cointreau

Serves 6

A gorgeous, rich dessert which looks a dream and yet can be made in as long as it takes to whip cream.

½pt (275ml) double cream
3 level tblsp caster sugar
2 tblsp Cointreau
1 tsp vanilla essence
1 can chestnuts in water (10oz or 275g), drained weight
1 large chocolate flake bar, crushed

163

1. Whip cream until thick with half the caster sugar. Fold in remainder with Cointreau and essence.
2. Break up chestnuts into smallish pieces. Stir gently into cream with a large metal spoon.
3. Transfer to 6 glass serving dishes and dust with crushed flake bar. Refrigerate 1 hour before serving.

Chestnut Coffee Cream

Serves 6

Make as above but substitute Tia Maria for Cointreau. Sprinkle with 1oz (25g) very finely-chopped pistachio nuts (or walnuts as they are less costly) instead of chocolate.

Cider Apple Fool

Serves 4 generously

With the apples simmered in cider and laced with Calvados (expensive here so bring some back when you next go to France!), this is a Fool with a difference and for adults only.

1lb (450g) cooking apples
3 tblsp sweet cider
3oz (75g) caster sugar
¼pt (150ml) canned custard (ready prepared)
1 tblsp Calvados (apple brandy)
¼pt (150ml) double cream
fresh mint leaves for decoration

1. Peel, core and slice apples and put into saucepan with cider. Bring to boil, lower heat and cover.
2. Simmer very gently for about 10 minutes or until apples become soft, pulpy and purée like.
3. Add sugar and stir over a low heat until dissolved. Cool. Stir

in custard and Calvados.

4. Beat cream until thick and fold into the apple mixture. When smooth and evenly blended, divide between 4 sundae glasses or bowls.

5. Chill about 2 hours. Decorate with mint leaves before serving.

Note

As an alternative to mint leaves, sprinkle tops with hundreds and thousands immediately before serving.

Satin Gooseberry Fluffs

Serves 6

Tangy, zesty and just the thing for balmy summer days. It is perfect just by itself or with some blackcurrant syrup trickled over the top; better still if the syrup happens to be Cassis!

1lb (450g) washed gooseberries, topped and tailed
3 tblsp water
4oz (125g) caster sugar
2 level tsp gelatine } mixed together and left to stand
5 tsp cold water   } 5 minutes
2 Grade 2 eggs, separated
green food colouring

1. Put gooseberries into saucepan with water. Cover. Bring to boil then lower heat. Cook slowly about 10 minutes or until fruit is soft and pulpy.
2. Remove from heat. Either beat until very smooth or mix to a purée in a blender or food processor.
3. Return to pan and add sugar with gelatine and water. Stir over a very low heat until sugar and gelatine have both melted.
4. Remove pan from heat, leave aside until lukewarm then beat in egg yolks. Tint pale green with food colouring. Cover. Refrigerate until just beginning to thicken and set.
5. Whisk egg whites to a stiff snow and gently fold into gooseberry mixture with a large metal spoon.
6. When smooth and evenly combined, spoon into 6 glass dishes and set in the refrigerator for about 6 hours.

Satin Rhubarb Froths

Serves 6

Make exactly as above, substituting 1lb (450g) rhubarb (trimmed weight) for gooseberries. Tint pink with food colouring if necessary.

Hungarian Sweet Noodles   *Serves 4*

The Hungarians love pasta-type dishes, and sweet noodles and nuts for a dessert dish make interesting eating.

8oz (225g) flat noodles
1oz (25g) butter
2oz (50g) walnuts, finely chopped
1½oz (40g) caster sugar
icing sugar

1. Cook noodles in boiling, salted water until just tender, allowing 7 to 10 minutes.
2. Drain and return to pan. Add butter, walnuts and caster sugar and toss with 2 spoons.
3. Transfer to 4 warm plates and sprinkle heavily with sifted icing sugar. Serve hot.

Note
In Hungary, the noodles would be tossed in lard but I find this makes them too greasy for my own personal taste.

Almond Pudding   *Serves 6 to 8*
with Apricot Sauce

A light and tempting steamed pudding, blanketed with a golden, fruity sauce.

8oz (225g) self-raising flour
4oz (125g) butter or margarine
2oz (50g) ground almonds
4oz (125g) caster sugar
2 Grade 3 eggs
½ tsp almond essence
about 6 to 7 tblsp cold milk to mix

Sauce
½pt (275ml) thick apricot purée, made from canned apricots
    thinned down with a little syrup
2 tblsp brandy, port or sherry

1. Well-grease a 3 pint (1¾ litre) pudding basin. Dust very
   lightly with extra ground almonds. Have ready a large
   saucepan for cooking the pudding.
2. Sift flour into a bowl. Rub in butter or margarine finely. Toss
   in almonds and sugar.
3. Beat eggs with essence. Add to dry ingredients then, using a
   fork, mix to a semi-stiff consistency with the milk. Stir briskly
   but do not beat.
4. Spread smoothly into prepared basin, cover securely with a
   double thickness of greased greaseproof paper or aluminium
   foil and put into saucepan.
5. Add sufficient boiling water to pan to come half way up sides
   of basin, then boil steadily for 2 hours.
6. Top up pan every so often with extra boiling water to keep
   up the level. Remove basin carefully from pan and invert on
   to a plate. Serve with the purée, heated through with the
   alcohol.

Blintzes

Makes 6

Mid-European and also highly esteemed in North America,
Blintzes are pancake bundles filled with a cottage cheese mixture
then parcelled up and fried in butter. Topped with spoons of

soured cream, these are a glutton's delight.

Pancakes
4oz (125g) plain flour
½ level tsp salt
1 Grade 2 egg
1 tsp salad oil (for velvety pancakes)
½pt (275ml) cold milk
fat for greasing pan

Filling
12oz (350g) cottage cheese
2 Grade 4 egg yolks
2oz (50g) caster sugar
1 tsp vanilla essence
1 level tsp finely-grated lemon peel
4oz (125g) butter, softened

Topping
sugar and cinnamon, mixed
soured cream

1. Sift flour and salt into a mixing bowl. Beat to a thick batter
   with egg, salad oil and half the milk.
2. Continue to beat until bubbles rise to the surface then gently
   fold in the rest of milk. Cover. Refrigerate about 4 hours.
3. Before frying, brush an 8 ins (20cm) heavy-based pan with
   melted white cooking fat. Heat until hot.
4. Pour in sufficient batter to cover base of pan thinly; about 4
   tablespoons. Fry on one side only, allowing it to turn light
   golden brown.
5. Place on damp tea towel, cooked sides down. Repeat, using
   up all the batter mixture to make 6 not-too-thin pancakes.
6. For filling, mix cheese with egg yolks, sugar, vanilla essence,
   lemon peel and 1oz (25g) butter.
7. Put on to centres of pancakes and parcel up by folding edges
   of each pancake over filling.

8. Sizzle remaining butter in frying pan then add pancakes, 2 or 3 at a time, with joins underneath. Fry until pale gold on both sides, turning twice.

9. Put on to 6 warm plates, sprinkle thickly with sugar and cinnamon then top each with soured cream. Serve straight away.

Pancake 'Parcels'

For an alternative filling, mix together 8oz (225g) cream cheese with 1 tablespoon Jif lemon juice and 2oz (50g) raisins. Serve the pancake parcels dusted with icing sugar and/or topped with soured cream.

Crepes Suzette   *Serves 6*

Make pancakes as above then fold each in four to resemble an envelope. Melt 4oz (125g) butter or margarine in large frying pan. Add 1oz (25g) sifted icing sugar, finely-grated peel and juice of 1 medium washed and dried orange, 1 level tsp finely-grated lemon peel and 4 tablespoons orange liqueur. Heat until bubbling. Add folded pancakes and heat through until hot, basting several times with the sauce. Heat a liqueur glass of brandy to lukewarm. Ignite and pour into pan over pancakes. Serve when flames have subsided.

Apple and Walnut Pancakes

Make pancakes as directed in recipe for Blintzes then fill with about 8oz (225g) sweetened apple purée, heated until hot with

1oz (25g) chopped walnuts. Dust with sifted icing sugar and serve hot.

Serve when flames have subsided

Queen of Puddings with Almond Crown

Serves 4

One of the most pleasant of old English puddings, this one has a ring of toasted flaked almonds to represent a crown by way of decoration and 'jewels' of glacé cherries.

3oz (75g) fresh white breadcrumbs
4oz (125g) caster sugar
1 level tsp finely-grated lemon peel
1 level tsp vanilla essence
¾pt (425ml) milk, heated to lukewarm
1oz (25g) butter or margarine, melted
2 Grade 3 eggs, separated
2 level tblsp raspberry jam, slightly warmed
1oz (25g) flaked almonds
6 glacé cherries halved

1. Put crumbs, 1oz (25g) sugar and lemon peel into a mixing bowl. Toss together to mix.
2. Beat vanilla essence with milk, butter or margarine and egg yolks.
3. Pour over crumbs, stir well and leave to stand for 30 minutes.
4. Spread smoothly into a 1½pt (¾ litre) greased ovenproof dish and bake 30 minutes just above oven centre set to 160°C (325°F), Gas 3.
5. Remove from oven and spread top with jam. Set aside temporarily.
6. Whisk egg whites to a stiff snow. Gradually beat in rest of sugar and continue beating until mixture is very thick.
7. Swirl over pudding, add a ring of the toasted almonds then stud with halved cherries.
8. Return to oven and bake a further 30 minutes when meringue should be pale gold. Serve hot.

Queen of Chocolate Puddings with Coconut

Serves 4

Make as above but melt 2oz (50g) plain chocolate in the milk while heating to lukewarm. Use brown crumbs instead of white and apricot jam instead of the raspberry. Sprinkle meringue with ½oz (15g) lightly toasted desiccated coconut.

Apple and Raisin Charlotte

Serves 4

A special edition, with the raisins first soaked overnight in sweet sherry.

2oz (50g) raisins
4 tblsp sweet sherry
1lb (450g) cooking apples
4oz (125g) light brown soft sugar
4oz (125g) fresh white breadcrumbs
finely-grated peel of 1 medium washed and dried lemon
3oz (75g) butter or margarine, melted

1. Put raisins into a small bowl, add sherry and toss well to mix. Cover and leave to stand overnight at kitchen temperature.
2. Peel and thinly slice apples. Mix together the sugar, crumbs and lemon peel.
3. Fill a 2 pint (just over 1 litre), well-greased heatproof dish with alternate layers of apples, raisins (plus any left over sherry) and breadcrumb mixture. Sprinkle butter or margarine between layers and end with crumb mixture.
4. Bake until apples are tender and top is golden and crusty, allowing about 45 minutes to 1 hour just above oven centre set to 190°C (375F), Gas 5.
5. Spoon on to plates and serve hot with cream or custard.

Gooseberry Amber

Serves 4

A golden oldie, useful for early summer gooseberries or, in the autumn, apples and blackberries.

1lb (450g) topped and tailed gooseberries, washed
1 tblsp water
1oz (25g) butter or margarine
7oz (200g) caster sugar
3 rounded tblsp cake crumbs (such as Madeira)
1 level tsp mixed spice
2 Grade 3 eggs, separated
½ tsp lemon juice

1. Put gooseberries into pan with water. Cover. Cook over minimal heat until soft and pulpy. Beat until smooth.
2. Mix in butter or margarine and 4oz (125g) sugar. Stir over a low heat until sugar dissolves.
3. Stir in cake crumbs, spice and egg yolks and lightly beat until well mixed.
4. Spread into a 1½ pint (1 litre) buttered heatproof dish.
5. Whisk egg whites to a stiff snow with lemon juice. Gradually beat in rest of sugar and continue beating until mixture is very thick.
6. Swirl over pudding then bake 30 minutes just above oven centre set to 160°C (325°F), Gas 3. Spoon out of dish and serve hot with cream or ice cream.

Apple and Blackberry Amber

Serves 4

Make as above, using 8oz (225g) *each* peeled and sliced apples (prepared weight) and blackberries.

174

Jam Sandwich Pudding   *Serves 4 to 6*

Bread and butter pudding in disguise, this time by making it with jam sandwiches.

12 large slices white bread, crusts removed
butter or margarine for spreading, at kitchen temperature
5 level tblsp plum jam
2 Grade 3 eggs
¾pt (425ml) milk
1 tsp vanilla essence
1oz (25g) Demerara sugar
1oz (25g) butter, melted

1. Spread slices of bread thickly with butter or margarine then sandwich together with jam.
2. Cut sandwiches into quarters and use to half-fill a 2½pt (1½ litre) buttered ovenproof dish.
3. Beat eggs with milk and vanilla essence then strain gently over sandwiches. Leave to stand 30 minutes at kitchen temperature.
4. Sprinkle with sugar then trickle 1oz (25g) butter over the top.
5. Bake until golden brown and crusty, allowing 45 to 50 minutes just above oven centre set to 180°C (350°F), Gas 4.
6. Spoon out of dish and serve hot with cream, custard or ice cream.

Marmalade Crinkle Slice   *Serves 6*

With coarse-cut marmalade tucked in the middle, this somewhat original pudding has a sophisticated and elegant air about it, yet is based on store cupboard ingredients which are not all that costly.

175

Pastry
8oz (225g) self-raising flour
4oz (125g) butter or margarine
4oz (125g) caster sugar
1 Grade 3 egg, beaten
milk if necessary

Filling
6oz (175g) coarse-cut orange marmalade

Topping
1 Grade 3 egg, beaten
1½oz (40g) cashews, fairly finely chopped
2 well-rounded tsp light brown soft sugar
2 tblsp double cream (taken from ¼pt or 150ml)

1. For pastry, sift flour into a bowl. Rub in butter or margarine finely.
2. Toss in sugar then, using a fork, mix to a fairly stiff dough with egg and extra milk if necessary. Draw together, form into a ball and foil-wrap. Chill ¾ to 1 hour or until firm.
3. Divide dough into 2 equal pieces and press one half over base of an 8 ins (20cm) greased sandwich tin. Spread with marmalade.
4. Using coarse side of grater, grate remaining dough over top of marmalade then brush thickly with beaten egg, applying it with a pastry brush.
5. Sprinkle with nuts and sugar then trickle over the cream. Bake 45 minutes in oven centre set to 200°C (400°F), Gas 6. Cut into 6 wedges and serve hot with cream or custard.

Apricot Crinkle Slice
Serves 6

Make as above, using whole fruit apricot jam instead of the marmalade.

No-Time-At-All Pudding

Serves 4 to 5

Baked in a loaf tin and served sliced with ice cream, this quickly-prepared fruit and spice pudding will make friends in no time.

6oz (175g) self-raising flour
½ level tsp cinnamon
½ level tsp ginger
½ level tsp mixed spice
¼ level tsp nutmeg
1½oz (40g) cooking dates, finely chopped
1oz (25g) brazil nuts, shaved into thin slivers
1½oz (40g) light brown soft sugar
1 level tsp finely-grated lemon peel
1 Grade 3 egg, beaten
¼pt (150ml) less 2 tblsp cold strained tea
1oz (25g) butter or margarine, melted

1. Well-grease and line a 1lb (450g) loaf tin. Set oven to 180°F (350°F), Gas 4.
2. Sift flour and spices into a bowl. Toss in dates, nuts, sugar and lemon peel.
3. Using a fork, mix to a softish consistency with egg, tea and butter or margarine.
4. Spread smoothly into tin then bake about 45 to 55 minutes just above oven centre. To test when ready, push a metal skewer gently into the centre. If it comes out clean and dry, pudding may be removed from the oven. If not, continue to bake a further 10 minutes.
5. Turn out into a dish, cut into thick slices and serve straight away with ice cream.

Pumpkin Pie

Serves 8 to 10

Eaten in America at Thanksgiving, Pumpkin Pie is easily made here at home from about October onwards when pumpkin starts appearing in the shops. It is well worth trying in that it has an unusual texture and fragrance and is mouthwatering with whipped cream.

about 3½lb (1¾kg) pumpkin
6oz (175g) light brown soft sugar
½oz (15g) cornflour
1 level tblsp black treacle
2 level tsp allspice
¼pt (150ml) canned and unsweetened evaporated milk
3 Grade 3 eggs, beaten
8oz (225g) shortcrust pastry made with 8oz (225g) flour and 4oz (125g) fat etc

1. Well-grease a baking tray. Set oven to 180°C (350°F), Gas 4.
2. Remove seeds and fibrous strings from pumpkin and discard. Put pumpkin on to tray, skin side uppermost.
3. Bake for about 1½ to 2 hours or until flesh is very soft. Remove from oven and spoon flesh into a bowl. Mash finely or mix to a purée in blender or food processor.
4. Spoon into a clean tea towel and squeeze dry. Put into bowl and beat in sugar, cornflour, treacle, allspice, milk and eggs.
5. Roll out pastry and use to line a 10 ins (25cm) flan tin standing on a greased baking tray. Trim edges to neaten then pinch between finger and thumb for a decorative finish.
6. Pour in pumpkin mixture and bake for about 45 to 55 minutes or until filling has set like an egg custard and the pastry is pale gold.
7. Remove from oven and lift off flan ring. Leave pie on tray for 5 minutes then carefully lift on to wire rack.
8. Cut into wedges when lukewarm and serve with ice cream.

Rhubarb Crumble with a Difference

Serves 4

A new-style crumble topping gives this rhubarb pudding a touch of individuality.

1lb (450g) rhubarb (trimmed weight), cut into 1 in (2½cm) lengths
2 tblsp water
2 rounded tblsp raspberry jam
2oz (50g) caster sugar

Crumble Topping
4oz (125g) plain flour
1oz (25g) porridge oats
2½oz (65g) butter or margarine
2oz (50g) light brown soft sugar
1 level tsp finely-grated lemon peel

1. Wash rhubarb pieces and put into a pan with water. Bring to boil, lower heat and cover. Simmer very gently for about 7 to 10 minutes or until soft and pulpy.
2. Beat in jam and sugar. Leave until cold. Put into 2 pint (1¼ litre) oval or round greased pie dish.
3. For crumble, sift flour into a bowl. Add oats then rub in butter or margarine finely. Toss in sugar and lemon peel.
4. Sprinkle thickly over fruit in dish. Bake about 20 minutes just above oven centre set to 200°C (400°F), Gas 6. Crumble is ready when it becomes light golden brown.
5. Spoon out of the dish and serve hot with cream, ice cream or custard.

Father Christmas Pudding

Serves 4 to 6

A mincemeat pudding with a difference, geared for yuletide eating.

8oz (225g) mincemeat
2 tblsp whisky
6oz (175g) self-raising flour
1 level tsp mixed spice
1 level tsp cinnamon
3oz (75g) butter or margarine
3oz (75g) light brown soft sugar
2oz (50g) flakes almonds, lightly toasted and coarsely crushed
½ tsp almond essence
1 Grade 3 egg ⎫
5 tblsp cold milk ⎬ beaten together

1. Mix together mincemeat and whisky and spread over base of 2 pint (1¼ litre) oval or round pie dish, first well-greased.
2. Sift flour, spice and cinnamon into a bowl. Rub in butter or margarine finely.
3. Toss in sugar and almonds. Mix to a softish consistency with the essence, egg and milk, stirring briskly with a fork.
4. Spread smoothly over mincemeat then bake 45 to 50 minutes in oven centre set to 190°C (375°F), Gas 5. The pudding is ready when a metal skewer, pushed gently into centre, comes out clean and dry.
5. Turn out on to a warm plate, cut into portions and serve hot with cream or custard.

Cocktail Choc Crumble

Serves 4

No one tires of crumble and this short-cut one has been a family

favourite for a long time, always welcome and predictably delicious. With its built-in custard, it needs no extras.

1 can (about 15oz or 425g) ready-to-serve custard
1 small can (about 8oz or 225g) fruit cocktail, drained
1 medium banana
4oz (125g) plain flour
½oz (15g) cocoa powder
2oz (50g) butter or margarine
2oz (50g) dark brown soft sugar

1. Set oven to 190°C (375°F), Gas 5. Butter a 2 pint (1¼ litre) pie dish.
2. Mix together custard and fruit cocktail. Slice in banana. Stir well. Spoon into pie dish.
3. For crumble, sift together flour and cocoa powder. Rub in butter or margarine. Toss in sugar.
4. Sprinkle smoothly over fruit and custard. Bake 30 minutes just above oven centre. Serve hot.

Note
Keep fruit syrups to sweeten blancmanges, white sauces for puddings and also to add to drinks. The syrup can also be used to moisten sponge cakes used for trifles.

Zabaglione
Serves 8

An entertaining dish and something you can whisk together in the kitchen while your guests are chatting. Also an Italian classic and a natural follow-on to a pasta meal.

8 Grade 1 or 2 egg yolks
8 level tblsp caster sugar
8 tblsp Marsala

1. Put egg yolks and sugar into a bowl resting over a pan of gently simmering water.
2. Whisk until mixture becomes thickish, foamy and pale in colour.
3. Add Marsala and continue to whisk until Zabaglione becomes more froth-like and lukewarm.
4. Pour into glasses and serve straight away. Accompany with crisp biscuits.

Enlightened Zabaglione   *Serves 8*

An economical version, where the egg whites are folded in to add bulk.

Make exactly as above but use 4 large eggs only. While Zabaglione is thickening over hot water, whisk egg whites and a squeeze of lemon to a stiff snow in clean and dry bowl. Add the Marsala to the yolk mixture then gently add the whites, beating as gently as you can all the time. When smooth and evenly combined, pour into 8 glasses or dishes and serve, with crisp biscuits, while still warm.

Zabaglione with Peaches   *Serves 6*
and Macaroons

Blanch 3 medium ripe peaches as you would blanch tomatoes then peel off skin under cold, running water. Cut in half and chop. Toss with 2 macaroons, first broken into small pieces, and 3 tablespoons brandy. Put into 4 glasses or bowls and pile high with warm Zabaglione. Serve straight away.

Apricot and Coconut Pudding   *Serves 4*

A typical family pudding, made for a topping of cream.

3 level tblsp apricot jam
4oz (125g) self-raising flour
2oz (50g) butter or margarine
2oz (50g) caster sugar
2oz (50g) desiccated coconut
1 Grade 3 egg, beaten
1 tsp vanilla essence
3 tblsp cold milk

1. Set oven to 180°C (350°F), Gas 4. Well-grease a 1½ pint (about ¾ litre) heatproof dish. Spread jam over base.
2. Sift flour into a bowl. Rub in butter or margarine finely. Toss in sugar and coconut.
3. Using a fork, mix to a softish consistency with the egg, essence and milk. Stir briskly but do not beat.
4. Spread smoothly into prepared dish over jam then bake 45 minutes just above oven centre.
5. Remove from oven and turn out on to a warm serving dish. Cut into 4 portions and serve straight away.

Syrup and Ginger Coconut Pudding   *Serves 4*

Make as above, substituting Golden Syrup for jam. Sift flour with 2 level teaspoons ginger and omit vanilla essence.

Cream of Creams

Serves 8

A Portuguese cream extravaganza which is unique unto itself. A variation follows, 'invented' by me.

3 Grade 1 or 2 egg yolks
4oz (125g) icing sugar, sifted
¼pt (150ml) double cream
1 carton (5oz or 150ml) soured cream
½ tsp vanilla essence
½ tsp almond essence (optional)
2 level tsp gelatine
2 tblsp cold water

Decoration
¼pt (150ml) double cream
1 large chocolate flake bar, crushed

1. Whisk egg yolks and sugar together until they become thick, creamy, almost white and paste-like.
2. Whip double cream until thick. Gently beat in soured cream. Fold creams into egg yolk mixture with essences. Refrigerate for the time being.
3. Put gelatine into small pan. Add water. Leave to stand 2 minutes. Melt over very low heat *but do not allow to boil.*
4. Cold to lukewarm then gently whisk into cream mixture. Pour into a shallow serving dish. Refrigerate several hours until set.
5. Before serving, whip cream and pipe or spoon on top of dessert. Finally sprinkle with chocolate flake bar.

Snowdrift Chocolate Cream

Serves 8

A stunner of a dessert to which melted white chocolate is added.

Make dessert exactly as above but add 4oz (125g) melted white chocolate (cooled) at the same time as the essences. When set, decorate with crystallised rose and violet petals.

Athol Brose

Serves 4

An unusual but imaginative sweet from Scotland, laced with the country's two staples — oats and whisky!

2oz (50g) porridge oats
3 tblsp whisky
2 level tblsp caster sugar
2 level tblsp heather honey
¼pt (150ml) double cream

Topping
1 level tblsp oats, lightly toasted under the grill.

1. Put oats, whisky, sugar and honey into a bowl. Mix well.
2. Whip cream until thick. Stir in the oat mixture. Divide equally between 4 glasses.
3. Sprinkle with toasted oats and chill lightly in the refrigerator before serving.

Exotic Fruit Salad

Serves 4

A de luxe fruit salad for summer eating.

1 level tblsp clear honey
½pt (275g) double cream, whipped
1 fresh pineapple, cut in half lengthwise
and flesh removed and chopped
1 small can (7oz or 200g) lychees, drained
1 orange, peeled and cut into segments
1 kiwi fruit, peeled and sliced

1. Fold the honey into the whipped cream.
2. Combine the chopped pineapple and other fruits with the cream mixture then pile into the pineapple half 'shells'.

188

Index

Index

Index